CALLING NEW DELHI
for *Free*

[AND OTHER EPHEMERAL TRUTHS OF THE 21ST CENTURY]

BY SUSAN KRAMER O'NEILL

A PEACE CORPS WRITERS BOOK

Calling New Delhi for Free
[And Other Ephemeral Truths of the 21st Century]
A Peace Corps Writers Book
An imprint of Peace Corps Worldwide
Copyright © 2013 by Susan Kramer O'Neill
For more information, contact peacecorpsworldwide@gmail.com.
Peace Corps Writers and the Peace Corps Writers colophon are
trademarks of PeaceCorpsWorldwide.org.
ISBN: 1-935-92533-4
ISBN-13: 978-1-935-92533-0
Library of Congress Control Number: 2013943535
First Peace Corps Writers Edition, July 2013

BOOK DESIGN AND COVER PHOTOGRAPH BY KRAMER O'NEILL

Just about everything in this book has been published on line in either my early Amazon author's blog, or in my present blog, *Off The Matrix*, on *Peacecorpsworldwide.org*, a zine for writers who served in the US Peace Corps. The exceptions: "The Surgeon's Little Helpers," which first saw light in 2000 in *Chattahoochie Review*, and was selected as a "Notable Essay of 2000" in the following year's *Best American Essays*; "The Shaman of Shimano; the Guru of Gears," which appeared as part of an article for *Adventure Cyclist* in 1999; and "Journey to the Underworld," which was published in December of 2001 in *The Vietnam War Generation Journal*.

Contents

Introduction

I'm typing this with my thumbs.

I just grabbed a Dunkin Donuts coffee and a French cruller (260 calories—they have to post it in New York City), which I consumed on the subway, and now I'm typing this on my iPhone in the tea lounge where I sit barefoot, waiting for my yoga class to begin.

Which says it all.

For now.

In the all-too-soon tomorrow, all this will be obsolete. Subways will be period pieces; donuts will be illegal. The iPhone, alas, is already old technology.

And yoga will, no doubt, be replaced by something that involves wires and leads and a handful of pills.

Technology is traveling at breakneck speed, dragging me along.

I thumb-typed the above in my old reporter's shorthand: *Im typn ths w m thms,* etc. My iPhone "corrects" what I write, turns it into whatever its little iPhone brain thinks I mean. Sometimes it really is correct: *Im* has become "I'm." Sometimes it's close: *ths* becomes "the."

Sometimes it's educational. *Cruller* becomes "crupper."

My NinjaWords app tells me that "crupper" is the rump of a horse.

——

I began writing a blog in 2006, when my husband and I lived in Andover, MA. Amazon.com offered me the space; it was easy, so I did it. I am primarily a fiction writer, but I once worked on weekly newspapers as a reporter—a profession that is now mostly obsolete. I wrote accounts of school and zoning boards and the odd feature story, and I also wrote a weekly column: odd essays about things that made me laugh or scratch my head or both.

A blog is what happens when a column becomes obsolete.

A few years ago, Amazon stopped archiving blog entries, which made the Amazon blog obsolete. I shifted my work to the welcoming arms of Peacecorpsworldwide.org, a terrific site for writers who, like me, had served in the Peace Corps (Venezuela, 1973-74, a country that, as I knew it, has become obsolete). According to the editor, my blog—titled *Off The Matrix* for reasons that can be divined from Googling *Non-Matrix Spouse*—"plans to explore the weird, multicultural world of NYC, and beyond, when the fancy strikes her, through the eyes of a newly-unassigned resident."

I have noticed that I have a penchant for writing about technology, and how its helter-skelter pace and inherent oddity affects our messy low-tech humanity. This was true when I had a column; now it's true of my blog entries. And why not? It's a broad topic, a far-reaching and twisted one. Technology, more often than not, is about change; conversely, these days, change is usually about technology. As are the permutations of change: the lack of change, the reaction to change, the refusal to change and, of course, our bumbling attempts to embrace change.

Newness is about technology. As, in many cases, is *oldness.* Communication is about technology. Travel and war are all about technology. Even when they're not—directly.

Maybe *everything* is about technology.

Whatever.

The essays here come from my blogs, or from the odd obscure literary magazine. Many of which are obsolete. You will probably notice that some of the pieces are set in Massachusetts and some in New York City; I moved from the former to the latter in early 2008. The essays are not in chronological order because I find chronological order boring. Deal with it.

This book comes with a disclaimer (What doesn't?): I do not hate technology. In fact, I am addicted to it. I am on Facebook; I have a Twitter account. I use an ATM, pay bills electronically, order sneakers on line. I write on computer. I read on Kindle. I take pictures, check the weather, plot directions, text my kids, listen to Red Sox games, read the paper, play Scrabble, WordWeaver and Words With Friends, amaze my grandkids with a virtual Zippo lighter, and type with my thumbs on my iPhone. I just wish it worked as a phone (Note to AT&T...).

Technology is everywhere, and it's on the march. Double-time. I use it; I love it; I need it.

But that doesn't mean it's not weird as a tripple-cruppered horse.

A Tall Tale

I had a battle today with a barista at Starbucks.

This was not the Starbucks I usually go to in the center of my town. Yes, there is a Starbucks in the center of my town; as George Carlin once said, "There's a Starbucks in my pants." However, today's Starbucks was a different one, next door to a movie theatre.

I had just watched a movie. It was a highly-touted comedy filled with fine actors playing characters who were supposed to be Loveably Quirky. After I watched it, I hit the Starbucks for some caffeine, a Tall (which is, I understand, Italian for "small") cappuccino, to wake me up.

The woman behind the counter was young and neatly dressed and looked like a college student. She was attractive, efficient and, as they say in Italian, Tall. She made me a Tall cappuccino in a paper cup.

She reached for a plastic lid.

"That's okay," I said. "I don't need a lid."

"You have to have a lid," she said. "It's company policy."

"Okay," I said, "then give it to me separately, rather than putting it on."

She narrowed her eyes at me. "I have to put it on. It's company policy."

"The Starbucks in the center of my town makes my cappuccino in a pottery cup," I said. "They don't even make lids for pottery cups. I'm sure you can just give it to me without the lid."

"I can't give it to you until I put a lid on it."

"I'm only going to take it off again to put cinnamon on top. Why bother to make me take it off?"

She clutched the drink tight, a hostage. "It's company policy. I have to put a lid on it."

"Look, if you're worried about my scalding myself, isn't there more chance of me spilling the coffee when I take off the lid than there is when you hand it to me? The lid locks onto the rim. It's not that easy to take it off."

Her face hardened and I could swear she grew menacingly Grande. She told me, in a tone reserved for small children who suffer from a devastating mental handicap, "I. Have. To. Put. The. Lid. On. Or. I. Can't. Give. You. The. Coffee."

She applied the plastic lid with a *snap*. It was the sound of triumph.

She handed it to me. I took one step to the condiment table, pried off the lid, and shook cinnamon on top of the foam. I threw out the lid.

I admired the drink. She had given it just the right proportion of foam to coffee, not always the case in Starbucks. Not even in the Starbucks in the center of my town.

I took a sip. Delicious. "It's perfect," I told the young woman. "Thank you."

She didn't seem to hear me.

In fact, she abruptly, precisely, turned her back on me.

Ah, god. I felt so...Tall.

[2006]

Is It Raining in Delhi?

Paul and I got each other a new printer for Christmas. A Kodak 5250.

We bought it at Staples before Christmas, but they had to order it. It would arrive after Christmas.

Which was fine; we had a full house for the holiday, and couldn't have made it to the desk to print without stepping on gifts, plates of hors d'oeuvres or miscellaneous O'Neills.

We received the printer the day before we were to leave for a week in Paris. Paul set it up.

Throughout our life together, I have always set up electronic gadgetry–not because I have outstanding skill in that realm, but because, unlike my husband, I read directions. So I held my breath while he programmed the printer. Then I installed the drivers on my computer.

He printed a picture from his iPad, using the printer's WiFi function. *Et voilà!* We shut it down, packed our bags and left.

A few days after we got back, I turned the printer on and attempted to print something. It made printy noises to no avail and told me there was a paper jam.

I opened the door to clear the jam. There was none.

I tried again. It told me the computer and the printer weren't communicating.

Maybe it was the paper, which was thick and stationary-ish?

I pulled on my boots and slogged four blocks through the snow to Walgreens, and bought a pack of HP printer/copier paper.

I fed it to the printer and tried again. Again, the faux jam. Again, the printer snubbed the computer.

It must be Paul's fault, I thought. I checked the settings on the printer. They were perfect.

I changed the ink cartridges. *Jam, jam, snub.*

I de-installed my drivers and downloaded new ones. The printer just glared at the computer, its WiFi light a malicious ice-blue.

"This printer is F**ked," I told Paul.

I called Staples the next morning. A woman asked when we'd bought the printer. I told her it was a Christmas present. Did I have the receipt? I assured her I did.

"Bring it in," she said.

It was raining; icy spears of sleet beat the snow to slush and turned the streets into rivers. We packed the printer in plastic bags, hustled it out into the morass, down the street to our car. We slewed off to the Coney Island Avenue Staples. We parked, climbed a desiccated snow bank, and dragged the printer down the flooded block and into the store.

I set it on the counter. *Drip, drip.*

A 12-year-old Staples tech glanced at it. "What brand?"

"Kodak."

He scratched a pimpled cheek. "You bought it when?"

I told him.

He checked his computer, shook his head, pointed to a sign on the counter titled Staples Easy Return Policy. "Too late. You had two weeks to return it."

It had been two weeks and four days.

"But I received it a week after I bought it," I said.

"That's not what our computer says."

"What can we do?" Paul asked him.

"Buy HP–we service that. You didn't, so call Kodak. Maybe they'll send you a new one."

We lugged the computer out into the rain, up the block, over the snowbank, into the car, back to the apartment. I hung my sopping coat on a chair and grabbed the phone.

I called Kodak. After ten minutes of *Your Call is Important to Us*, I spoke to Sunil in New Delhi. I described my printer's woes at length.

A pause. Then he said, "You have a paper jam?"

I described my printer's woes very, very slowly.

"This error message–it says you have a paper jam?"

I sighed.

Under Sunil's guidance–as he consulted an instruction manual in Hindi that told him how to work with Macs–I de-installed my drivers, downloaded and re-installed them. *Jam, snub.*

I downloaded firmware, whatever the hell that is. *Jam, jam. Snub.*

An hour passed.

It printed. One page, crooked and crumpled. Then it jammed.

"Please take off the back door and see if there remains orange tape there or above the paper tray," Sunil said. His tone added, *Stupid American woman.*

Oh, Paul, I thought. *Tell me you didn't leave orange tape–*

There was none.

We tried again. *Jam, jam, jam, snub.*

Sunil put me on hold. My phone battery died.

I answered his call-back on our extension phone. "My supervisor has one question," he said. "What paper do you use?"

I told him I used HP printer paper.

"Please try it with Kodak printer paper," he said.

I ground my teeth. "Hewlett-Packard is excellent paper, not some off-brand," I said. "We both know all these papers are made in the same factory in China. You want me to throw on a raincoat and *drive to Staples and buy a pack of Kodak paper? Come on!* If this machine is so temperamental I have to hand-feed it Kodak paper–"

"Yes, yes, They all come from the same factory." Sunil was the soul of rationality. "Still, Kodak printers should be used with Kodak paper."

I grunted something that must've sounded dubious–or perhaps threatening–and he quickly added, "However, Kodak is willing to send you a new printer…"

I gave him my address and hung up.

He called back. "I cannot make your address match the records."

He had written Brookline instead of Brooklyn. He made the correction and hung up.

He called again: The address still didn't compute. He had inverted two numbers in the zip code.

I stayed on the phone while he entered the data. No luck. He had misspelled *Avenue*. He made the correction.

We hung up–for the last time, I hoped.

Et…voilà?

I glanced at the clock. It had taken me two hours and five minutes, two phones and four calls to convince Kodak what I'd realized the day before:

My new printer was F**ked.

[2011]

The Safe Baby

I have one grandchild, my daughter's son, a funny, intense little boy who is 20 months old. Little Grey has a vocabulary of three words: *Ma, Dad,* and *No.*

Ever the writer, I try to introduce him to new words. *No,* he tells me. The inflection is uncompromising.

Someday he will speak in sentences, I suspect. But for now, maybe *No* is not a bad thing.

There are so many things for a child to say *No* to in these troubled times.

There are predators, drug pushers, peanut butter and Pre-school Interviews. It's not easy being a child.

Nor is it easy, these days, to be a parent. You have all of the above, to begin with. Then there's the heavy equipment.

The convenient umbrella stroller I used for my kids? The lightweight car seat? The wooden high chair? All banned as unsafe.

Children are now awash in safety. They're swamped with it. Their safety begins at home, but their parents also must portage it onto subways, into cars, on trains, buses and planes.

Shortly after Grey was born, I went shopping for a sling so I could carry him when he came to visit. I went to Babies R Us.

Big-box department stores creep me out. The sheer volume of inventory strikes me catatonic. I walked through the door of

Babies R Us, and a ceiling-high maze of Absolutely Essential Equipment pressed in on me. Air-blocking bottles, industrial-strength perambulators with built-in strait-jackets, fifty-pound car seats, backpacks with roll-bars and sun-shields, body-molded shoulder-harness high chairs, cribs with slats three inches apart, bumpers to keep baby from a deadly roll onto her tummy, intercoms to broadcast every hiccup.

Every last item was plastered with warning labels.

Choking hazard! Do not leave side down! Do not prop baby! Do not hang baby from hook! Remove plastic cover! Not for infants under six months! Not for internal consumption! Do not permit baby to gnaw cord! Do not throw electric warmer in bathtub!!!

I began to hyperventilate. A 14-year-old stock clerk with a spear through her eyebrow caught me as I swooned; she slapped my cheeks and passed my credit card under my nose to revive me. "You can do it, man," she rasped, and pushed me through an arch made of boxed Barbie Dolls, into the Child Portation department.

I last bought a baby sling when my youngest was born. He's now 26. His sling was cotton, folded to fit in my diaper bag, and adjusted with a simple metal buckle. I bought it in a drug store. You can no longer find it; it has been banned as unsafe.

In Babies R Us, there were three Personal Baby Carriers. The first was a front pack that had to be assembled by an ambidextrous mechanical engineer. The second was a rip-proof reinforced nylon hip-tote with five padded straps.

The third was a real sling.

I mean a *real* sling. A wonder of a thing: a great, heavy sheet of multi-layered hypoallergenic cloth with foam-padded borders and an indestructible steel buckle. A stout cloth tail threaded through this buckle and terminated in a little plastic log. The log was a failsafe: it would catch on the buckle if the wearer were caught in a tornado that pulled the tail through the steel loops and threaten to spill the baby onto the floor.

This sling was designed by a doctor. I found that reassuring, since doctors spend so much time carrying babies around.

I bought it. I brought it home and unpacked it. Enclosed was a videotape on how to use it.

Baby Grey hated the sling. If he were able to speak at that point in his infancy, he would have said *No*.

Perhaps I was misusing the contraption, since I had not viewed the videotape. Perhaps he mistook the sling's hefty comfort for unnecessary heat and bulk. Perhaps the ultra-safe foam-padded edges made him feel claustrophobic when they closed safely over his face.

Perhaps it was because the first—and last—time I carried him in it was when I went to New York to visit him, when he was two months old, and we took him to a Yankees/Red Sox game in Yankee Stadium. Perhaps even the multi-layered hypoallergenic cloth and the foam-rubber padding were not stout enough to shield his infant ears from my cries of anguish when Boston lost.

Whatever the case, the equipment was clearly too sophisticated for my use. It was Safety Incarnate, and I was a flawed human. A failure. We returned to Massachusetts after our visit, and the sling marched off under its own power—it was that formidable—and took refuge in our attic.

I have not seen it since.

[2006]

Of Ants and Men

I opened our garage door last week and noticed piles of sawdust.

The garage is big enough for one car. If we were to use it for a car. Which we don't, because it's the only place we can store the bikes.

There are two of us, but we have seven bikes. Paul and I each have one. The rest are Frankensteins I assembled from parts for the kids when they were younger, back when I taught myself bicycle mechanics in case I needed to repair mine on the road. The kids have moved on; the bikes have stayed.

Anyway: I opened the garage door and there were piles of sawdust on the floor and on the seats of the bikes. Which was curious, because nobody ever engages in woodworking in our garage. There's no space for it, what with all the bikes, and no light. Except, perhaps, for the sunlight that was filtering through the little holes in the roof.

Which was also curious, because there weren't supposed to be little holes in the roof.

I called an exterminating company to come out and take a look. They sent Eric, a very tall and amiable young man from Cameroon who was educated in Italy and speaks six languages.

Eric examined the sawdust. "Madame," he said, "you have carpenter ants."

I trailed after him as he walked our postage-stamp lot. "You must trim back these trees," he said. "You must cut these bushes. That is how the ants come to your wood."

Messing with green and growing things makes my skin break out in little bumps. I know nothing whatsoever about lawns, trees and bushes. Paul's equally clueless, but he's an alpha male, so every now and then he declares war upon our foliage. He pulls on leather gauntlets, assembles clippers, trimmers, saws and mowers, and hacks his way through the underbrush. Very often, things that he trims do not grow back. Ever. I call his approach to yard work the Massachusetts Chainsaw Massacre.

When I look at our yard, with its piebald turf, overgrown trees and hacked-up bushes, I am amazed that the neighbors haven't strung us up. My father, may he rest in peace, would weep; we would never be permitted to own a home in Indiana.

But back to Eric the exterminator. He told me with great gravity, "You must promise me that you will trim every bush until it is a foot and a half away from the house."

I heaved a great sigh.

He said, "You can do it. You are a fine, strong woman. Hard work is good for you."

He then talked me into buying his company's self-renewing plan for elimination of carpenter ants, not only from the garage, but from the house, as a preventative measure. Spoken in Eric's lilting, formal English, the deal didn't sound bad: A little spray here—"We will only put it in the cracks, you understand." A little bait there—"It will do no harm to children or pets, of course. It is a very small concentration." The industry, he assured me, is regulated very tightly by the federal government—

I remarked that this is the same federal government that regulates my phone privacy and the specs on levees in New Orleans, as well as the concentration of mouse turds permitted in hot dogs.

Whereupon we launched into a discussion of our respective monarchies and their imperfections. Governments, we agreed at length, are messy and inefficient, often ineffective, and seldom exist for the good of the governed.

"Does it bother you," I said, "that we both know of a governing system that is tidy, efficient, effective and operates with maximum benefit to all its subjects, and your job is to kill it?"

"That is true," he said, "but it is eating your garage."

I signed the contract on the ants—which also covered a long list of other bugs, some of which are only found where Eric grew up—and he ducked around the house and garage, into the bathrooms and the kitchen, anointing crannies with government-regulated poisons.

Now Eric is gone, the tree-and-bush man is coming on Friday, and I am trying to live with the consequences of my actions.

It disturbs me that I have ordered this wholesale slaughter, however justified. I've been a vegetarian for 20 years because I consider animals sentient beings and don't like to kill them. My concern doesn't stop with the cute, furry ones: I've relocated mice, studied with fascination the spiders that work the corner of our bathroom, even ferried big black ants out of the kitchen and into the back yard. Yes, those ants—carpenter ants.

Now…I'm annihilating them.

My moral compass is spinning out of control.

This morning, while I was peeling a boiled egg at my kitchen counter, an ant crawled out from under the blender. I grabbed a napkin, intent on picking it up and giving it a ride into the yard, as I had so many of its cohorts. Back when there *were* many of them. Back before I unleashed Eric and his government-regulated devastation upon their clan.

I bent close and examined the creature. It did not run away. It moved slowly and somewhat erratically.

It was…staggering.

I laid down my napkin and watched the ant wander off beneath the coffee maker. I didn't have the heart to make its last days even more miserable.

[2006]

The Shaman of Shimano; the Guru of Gears

It was the 11th day of our bike ride from Hanoi to Ho Chi Minh City, Viet Nam. I was peddling the outskirts of Nha Trang with two fellow cyclists, Russell and Bill, when Bill's bike got a flat tire. We pulled over on a cracked sidewalk; I took out my tire repair kit and we wrenched the wheel off.

The entire population of the nearest hamlet materialized, as if summoned. Men, women and children, they gathered around us, waiting for the show to begin.

A man arrived, carrying a little boy who was naked beneath a T-shirt. We could tell the man was the Bike Shaman because his child was teething on a coil of new brake cable. He watched in silence, cigarette drooping from the corner of his mouth, as we set a new inner tube into the tire, then tried to inflate it with the shiny, high-tech pump Russell carried clipped to his bicycle frame.

Nothing happened.

We shifted the wheel, re-attached the pump, tried again. Again. Again. The tire remained flat.

The crowd fell back and the Bike Shaman stepped forward. He flicked his cigarette into the gutter and set his little son down on the sidewalk. An Acolyte handed him a battered old pump: the enamel on the housing had rusted from red to brown, and it was scratched and pockmarked. The rubber was worn off its handles. The threadbare hose had long ago lost its nozzle. The Bike Shaman stuck its frayed distal end over the state-of-the-art pressor valve on Bill's new inner tube, clamped it in place with his fingers, and pumped.

He nodded his head, doctor-like—*um-hum, um-hum*—as the air escaped. He dexterously removed the tire once again with my spoons, pulled out the inner tube, re-attached his nozzle-less hose, pumped, listened.

He isolated a new leak.

He stretched the tube over the handle of his sad old pump and whacked a little patch from my repair kit into place, using Russell's shiny high-tech frame pump as a mallet.

The Bike Shaman re-pumped the tube with his old rig. *Fsssss.* He cocked his head and listened, located yet another hole—this was a brand-new tube, which says something about the manufacturer's Quality Control—and patched it as he had the first.

Fsssssssh. Another hole.

The baby, who was now teething on Russell's shiny high-tech frame pump, squatted and urinated on the sidewalk.

Bill dug another new tube out of his pack. The Bike Shaman installed it, put the tire back on, inflated it with his ratty old nozzle-less pump, and stood back to admire his handiwork.

The crowd around us leaned in, holding its collective breath.

The air held.

The audience exhaled, nodded, smiled, talked amongst themselves. Bill paid the Bike Shaman 10,000 Dong, the requisite fee for the service.

The Bike Shaman lifted his son to his hip. He handed the boy the coil of new brake cable, and the baby dropped Russell's high-tech frame pump on the sidewalk.

One of the onlookers picked it up. He hefted the Bike Shaman's old pump in his other hand. He pocketed Russell's shiny high-tech frame pump, and made a show of tying the Bike Shaman's rusty old pump onto the bike by its ratty hose.

The crowd hooted. Russell held out his hand; grinning like a jester, the man laid the high-tech pump in his palm.

We rode away—with Bill's tire intact and Russell's high-tech pump once again clipped to his bike's frame—trailed by the whooping and chortling of the entire population of the nearest hamlet.

[1999]

A Humblig Bobent

I have a terrible cold, and I know exactly where I got it.

It wasn't from that guy on the subway. You know that guy; he stands next to the door and gives a little...*sniff*... barely audible, nothing blatant like the guy in the seat picking his nose. So subtle you don't even think about it, until you're at the door beside him, ready to leave, and he sneezes all over you.

It wasn't him.

It was from a kid at the clinic where I volunteer as a reader and wild-kid-wrangler.

I got it by being Entirely Too Clever.

Most kids come to the clinic for well-child physicals and immunizations. There are a few who look feverish and exhausted, but they don't come to me; they cling to their parents. Who will soon look feverish and exhausted.

Some kids do have colds. Colds don't get no respect; if the kid's scheduled to be weighed, measured and needled, mom brings him in, cold and all.

Who can blame her? Kids swap colds at school all week; why is a clinic any different?

As a former nurse, I take standard precautions to protect myself from drippy-nosed tots. I wash my hands. I use hand-sanitizer. If somebody's drawing in his snot with the blue crayon, blue does not return to my box.

But this four-year-old boy caught me up while I was being Entirely Too Clever.

He was bored. We'd read, drawn and colored, and the doctor still hadn't called him. He squirmed and sniffled and wiped his nose on his sleeve. I felt sorry for him.

So I pulled out my iPhone.

You know those TV ads about iPhone apps? I have some dazzlers. What's that song playing in the elevator? I'll ask my Shazam. I've got an app to flash LOSER, in three-inch neon-green running letters, at the Subway Sneezer as he pulls away from the platform. I've got a level tool with a bubble. Yelp. Facebook. Scrabble.

And I have Balloonanimal. Blow into the phone receiver: it inflates a picture of a long green balloon. Shake it, it twists into a dinosaur. Hit a pump icon, pump it up, up, up: *Blam*.

I showed the kid Balloonanimal.

No, I did not let him blow into my iPhone. I'm no idiot. I blew it up myself. Pumped it up. Popped it.

He jumped up and down. *Do it again!* I did. *Do it again!* I did.

The third time, he brought his face near the popping balloon and laughed, his mouth wide open.

Then he sneezed all over it.

There is no way to clean an iPhone with hand-sanitizer. And you can't get them wet, so soap and water's a no-no—although a little on a paper towel rids the glass of streaks left by hand-sanitizer.

I've got a horrible cold. But I've also got a learning curve. From now on, we stick to crayons and books.

[2009]

Commemorating
the Dread

Every Christmas, I hand-craft ornaments from acrylic clay to give to relatives and friends. Each ornament represents something important that happened in my life during the year. The year my story collection first came out, I made devils reading books. I've commemorated each grandkid's birth—Grey's baby figure wore a Red Sox cap, a two-fer because he was born in 2004.

So…this year's ornament is a bedbug.

Bedbugs are the current fashion in NYC. They've graced the cover of the *New Yorker*, popped up in city offices, stalked Victoria's Secret, and been discovered in shock-jock Howard Stern's studio (Seth Meyers, on *Saturday Night Live* news: "'This is disgusting,' said the bedbugs."). Venerable, regally-overpriced Bergdorf Goodman keeps a bedbug-sniffing beagle in the store to reassure personal shoppers that their clients' Gucci won't be itchi. Visitors to posh Manhattan hotels keep their luggage in the bathrooms. Even homeless New Yorkers no longer adopt abandoned mattresses off the sidewalk.

Our building's exterminator warns us to bring flashlights to movie theatres. "You shine 'em on the seat and check out every seam," he says. "Every inch. You check the seats on either side, and in front and back. You get home, you stand in the bathtub, strip, shake off all your clothes. They can't crawl outa of the tub—too steep, y'know?"

Our management company hires the exterminator primarily to eliminate what Brooklynites call waterbugs, which are to cockroaches what Shaq is to WeeMan. Every month, the guy puts a dab of goo in each of our cupboards. We never had waterbugs in our cupboards until after he started doing this. I'm not sure I would hire him to exterminate bedbugs if I had them.

Although our downstairs neighbors claim he did a decent job with theirs.

The downstairs neighbors moved in last Spring—a young couple with a toddler. I welcomed them with a plate of cookies.

Their first week, they noticed teensy reddish-brown bugs in their new apartment. Were these baby cockroaches? They checked them out on the Internet.

They weren't.

I ran into my new neighbor in the courtyard, and she sheepishly confessed that they had bedbugs. Sheepishly, because bedbugs are the Leprosy of 21st century New York. Friends shun you. People don't invite you to dinner. They never, *never* come to visit.

My neighbor told me the van carrying their furniture from their old—bedbug-free—apartment must've been infested. "I thought of you and felt terrible," she said. "I thought, *She gives me cookies; I give her bedbugs.*"

If you have cockroaches in New York, you put dabs of goo in your cupboards. If you have moths, you clean out your closets and scatter moth balls or cedar. If you have carpet beetles, you dry clean and use insecticides. If you have mosquitoes, you spray chemicals and slather yourself with Off. If you have head lice, you shampoo, run a nit comb through your hair, wash your linen, air your pillows. If you have fleas, you spread flea powder, vacuum, spray and put drops of poison on your pet's neck.

If you have bedbugs, you get an exterminator. Then you throw out your upholstered furniture, mattresses, bedding, drapes, carpeting—plastic-wrapping everything before you haul it to the curb. You encase new mattresses in pricy BedBugBags and duct-tape the zippers. You wash clothes in scalding water, seal dry-cleanables in plastic bags with bug killer, run luggage, books, toys, shoes, and *objets d'art* through a special heat unit. You scrub, vacuum, calk. Then you bring in a bedbug-sniffing dog, if you can find one who's not occupied at Bergdorf-Goodman, to make sure you're clean.

Bedbugs are the most expensive critters in New York to get rid of. They are also, of the bugs listed above, the most innocuous. Bedbugs bite, but they don't give you diseases. They make you itch, and hitchhike in your suitcase, but they don't try to become a permanent part of your body. They don't eat your winter coat or your Orientals.

They're just...icky.

My chat with my new neighbor gave me bedbug nightmares. I woke in the wee hours sweating, digging at imaginary bites.

After three nights of this, I stopped at the hardware store. I bought a spray called *Kills Bedbugs II*, and a tub of *Kills Bedbugs Powder*—diatomaceous earth, a natural compound used in swimming pool filters. I also bought a suitcase spray.

"Wow," the checkout girl said.

"I don't have bedbugs," I said.

"Sure."

"Seriously. It's my neighbor."

"Right." She took my money.

"My neighbor downstairs. This is preventative."

"Uh huh." Was that a smirk? She handed me my bag. "Spray under your door."

"Oh?"

"Keeps 'em from spreading." Definitely a smirk. "From those *neighbors*."

Paul and I spent the next day hip-deep in chemicals. He sprayed the room margins and every crack in the floor and the walls with *Kills Bedbugs II*. I took apart every electrical outlet and switch plate and puffed *Kills Bedbugs Powder* inside, then capped the outlet holes with childproof shields to keep them dry. I threw powder behind the refrigerator, beneath the heaters and under the cupboards. I sprayed the hell out of our suitcases.

I even sprayed under the damned door.

———

I've seen no evidence of bedbugs. The building's hired exterminator checked out all of our units and pronounced them clean.

My new neighbor is nervously optimistic, although she and her husband still sleep on a futon, and they run everything that comes into the apartment through their special heat unit.

I plan to make the poor souls some Christmas cookies soon. I'll also bring them a hand-crafted ornament.

Although...I'm not sure they'll want it.

[2010]

What's Wrong With This Picture?

I have here on my desk a picture of my youngest child, dressed in US Army desert fatigues and clutching the leash of an attack dog named Kevin.

There is so much wrong with this picture, I don't know quite where to begin.

Maybe with the dog.

Kevin is a sleek, shepherd-ish animal, all sinew and radar ears—one impressive-looking attack dog.

But Kel has never liked dogs. I've never seen him stop to pet one. He has never asked for a puppy. Those scenes in *A Fish Called Wanda*, when yippy little Yorkies get squished by falling safes? Had him in stitches. I can't imagine him playing fetch.

So the dog's wrong.

And what kind of twisted cynic would name an attack dog *Kevin*?

As it turns out, the folks at Blackwater, who trained him, named him Kevin.

Blackwater offers, to quote its website, "...comprehensive professional military, law enforcement, security, peacekeeping and stability operations... Vision: to support security, peace, freedom, and democracy everywhere."

And to train attack dogs. And to train my son to use an attack dog. And an M16.

Blackwater are, in short, mercenaries paid by the government to dance some of the fancy footwork of war. They are not a new concept, and they raise eyebrows for a variety of reasons: their pay, far healthier than their Army counterparts'; their far-right über-Christian political roots; their connection with "black holes" where our war prisoners are "interrogated"; their monetary links to certain powerful men in our government, to name a few.

Some people feel that war profiteering done by folks like Blackwater is Wrong. I must admit, knowing my taxes are paying for them and, now, that they're dealing with my son…it makes me itch.

Moving on:

The uniform is wrong. Desert fatigues, helmet and sand goggles are right for a US Army soldier, but for Kel?

Kel's not a GI, but he plays one in a movie. It's a movie that deals intimately with Wrong: it's based on the case of soldiers recently found guilty of raping an Iraqi girl and murdering her family.

The act was a grievous Wrong that underscores a fundamental, horrible irony of war: that even in a world where pathology is the norm, there are pathologies that cannot be tolerated.

What I mean is this: the purpose of war is to kill and wreak havoc. Governments won't tell you this in so many words; recruiters tend to gloss it over with mottos like *Army Strong*. But in war, people are expected to shoot people, blow up them and their property, drop bombs on them and their cities. The planned end result of these actions is to kill and wreak havoc. It's the Mission, however unpublicized, of war, through which the *stated* mission—freedom and democracy, perhaps—is accomplished.

This is not to denigrate individuals in the military. Individually, most members of the military, even volunteers, would likely prefer to not kill and wreak havoc; individually, a soldier is likely to consider doing so strictly a matter of self-defense.

The average soldier wants to believe he's in the field to win hearts and minds, to spread freedom and democracy. But if that's truly his Mission, does he need an M16, hand grenades and an attack dog named Kevin?

Whatever the motive or the rationalization, the Right or Wrong, the Mission of war demands actions that would be considered pathological in the "normal" world. If I lurk in an alley in Peoria looking for people who disagree with whatever my stated philosophy might be and if, when I find them, I kill them before they can kill me (or even if I just sic Kevin on them), I would wind up in jail.

In war, that scenario is the norm, and often merits decoration.

It is against this landscape that rape and murder can take on a weird irony.

Rape and murder are terrible things. And cloaking rape and murder in the chaos of war is not new; Shakespeare wrote about it, and it certainly predated Macbeth. It's just that, *when you consider the Mission*, can we really be outraged when an Abu Graib, or a case of rape and murder, or a My Lai Massacre (Google it, young readers) raises its hideous head during a war?

Certainly, most soldiers are fine people. But the Mission can present a veritable playground for the few who are psychopaths.

So…The subject of the movie Kel's filming is all about Wrong.

The fact that it's being filmed now, with the war still in play, with the wounds of all involved—the perpetrators, their families, the victims' families and all those people connected by life's sticky threads to the killers and the dead—still raw…well…

Granted, the world moves quickly these days, and every juicy disaster becomes a TV special within months after it hits the headlines; granted, wrongdoings financed by the government at our expense *should* be brought to light. But: there's a profit motive beneath the making of a movie like this that feels a little…Blackwater. A bit glib, like naming an attack dog Kevin.

A tad…Wrong.

However. The man in this picture on my desk is my son, an actor. He works hard at his craft, often for little pay. He's good at what he does. As his mother, I want him to achieve what he's fighting so hard for: To be able to eat regularly and well. To pay his rent. To help support his family. To pay his shrink bills (as I said, he's an actor).

I am in awe of his ambition, his perseverance, his drive, his willingness to put his ego and appearance and talent on the line with every audition. As a much-rejected author, I have some appreciation for the flexibility and strength such things require.

Now, as his reward for all this, he has been immortalized in desert fatigues, in the company of an attack dog. Named *Kevin*, for goddsakes. And this role will pay for the above-mentioned food, rent, support, maybe even the shrink bills. It is, for him, a good thing. A Right thing.

For my part, I am obscenely glad that this picture is not reality, that the young man in it, who is dear to me, will come home soon. That he will put this behind him and go on to other projects. That if it gives him nightmares, they will not be about the real horror of making real moral choices that could haunt him for the rest of his life.

This is not true of many young people in that uniform. They're off in Iraq or Afghanistan for real—sometimes for years at a time—risking their lives, their health and their futures for a dubious mission ordered by men who have never had to personally negotiate war's bizarre moral switchbacks. Men who play a role with borrowed jungle fatigues. Kind of like what my son is doing.

But Kel's an actor, playing a fictional soldier. These men—these dubious leaders—are not. The role they play is God.

And that, to me, is the most egregious Wrong of all.

[2007]

Charlie Accepts the Mark

I stepped out of the train from New York on Monday and into Future-World. It was not pretty.

Amtrak runs from New York Penn Station to Boston's South Station. The Red Line subway, which I'd ride to get to the commuter rail home, stops in the basement of South Station. I took the escalator downstairs from Amtrak, pulled out a token to drop in the turnstile—

And discovered that there was no slot for it.

There had been slots when I left last week, I was sure of it.

I rushed from turnstile to turnstile. No token slots. None.

I must've looked like one of those panicked subway rats that bump from track to track when they hear the train coming, because a strange man took me by the elbow and steered me to a bank of machines next to the entrance. He asked me, in a cheerful Mr. Rogers voice, *Do you have cash?*

I've been asked that question before in South Station, but not by somebody who looked like he'd recently had a bath. This man was not only clean, he was wearing a brand-new MBTA uniform and hat.

I stared at the machine and its shiny buttons and flashing lights. The Helpful Subway Man asked me again—*Cash?*

I held up my token, and he nearly clapped. *You can use that, too,* he exclaimed. He pointed to the machine. I could drop my token in *there—Yes, yes, do it.* Then you touch *this*, push *this*—

I lifted the token up to the slot, but it wouldn't leave my fingers. I couldn't do it. I couldn't exchange this solid token for that flimsy new magnetized disposable paper subway pass.

I'd only been gone a weekend. Was this the work of diabolical nocturnal elves?

In fairness, Boston must be the last city in the universe to scrap the token. You might say they gave it a fair run, considering the city sent its first train underground in 1897, which made it the first real subway system in the country. I'll bet if I called the MBTA—formerly the MTA, made famous by a 1948 campaign song wherein Progressive Party mayoral candidate Walter O'Brien pledged to save Charlie from a fare increase that made him ride forever 'neath the streets of Boston—some Helpful Subway Man would insist they were adopting the new system (dubbed—oddly, considering his fate—the "Charlie Pass") to make things more efficient, streamlined and cost-effective. And I dunno, even though some Luddites might question why a perpetually-broke MBTA is spending 200 million bucks to become cost-effective, maybe that Helpful Subway Man would be right.

I am an old lady, and I'll admit that I'm leery of this all-pervasive efficient magnetic information technology. My problem with this particular change really doesn't have a thing to do with that flyer a guy in Brooklyn handed me this weekend exhorting me to *Refuse the Mark of the Beast at All Costs!* It doesn't have to do with the tree-killing, litter-promoting disposability of the new tickets. It doesn't have to do with waiting in line at confusing vending machines—which will probably malfunction and break down just like they do in New York or DC—or even with the unemployment of erstwhile token venders.

It has to do with…touch.

The token is like a coin, round and substantial. Stick it in your pocket, and it won't bend; it will pass through the laundry or your pet Rotweiller and come out unaltered. Practically the only way you can render it useless is to place it on a subway track, which isn't easy, from five feet above. Unlike the Charlie Ticket, as fragile as a playing card, a token is dependable, trustworthy, cool to the touch. It's a tactile experience.

Furthermore, to buy one, you have to come face-to-face with a seller in a little booth. That's not always an unmixed delight— I've bought tokens from an old man who communicated in grunts and from a women talking on her cell phone—but it's a human encounter.

I can go through an entire day without a meaningful human encounter, without putting something into, or receiving something from, a human hand. My YMCA checks me in by scanning a little plastic card on my key-ring, so I can go work out on my individual machine. I stick my credit card into a gas pump, and never deal with an attendant. The mail carrier shoves my mail through the slot in my door; if there's something important, I email my husband at his office to let him know. If my Boston Globe goes missing, I settle the issue with an automated voice by tapping my phone's keypad. There is even a machine in the big grocery down the street that scans each banana and can of tuna, then takes my money or credit card via a magnetized slot.

If it weren't for the coffee shop in the middle of town, I might become a roaming Boo Radley.

And so I mourn the passing of one more human encounter. And the passing of one more object that feels good in the fingers, something small and pleasing and more permanent than a piece of paper. Something that works mechanically—you drop it into a slot, there's a metal-on-metal *tink*, and gears unlock.

After the Helpful Subway Man finally coaxed the token from my fingers and into the machine, I rode the Red Line to the Green Line and emerged, at last, at the North Station T-stop. I pushed through the exit turnstile.

It still had a token slot.

There was a booth, with a young woman inside. It seemed the MBTA hadn't extended Future-World to its old and funky Green Line.

Not yet.

I had a commuter train to catch, but...

I took my place in line.

I reached the woman. I gave her a smile and a $10 bill.

She gave me eight tokens. Eight shiny little gold-colored metal disks, cool and slightly heavy in my hand, each stamped with a "T" on one side and an etching of a subway car on the other.

When I got home, I put them in a jar.

I will bring them out and hold them someday, when I need the world to slow down.

[2006]

From Russia, Hold the Love

It was a coal-fired train, black smoke chuffing from a pipe on top, and it left at 11:25 p.m. from the ornate Vitebsk station in St. Petersburg, Russia. We sat in a second-class compartment with four pull-down cots. We had the compartment to ourselves.

I stowed my bag beneath my bunk; Paul wedged his against the table. In most trains, the little table beneath the window folds back to leave more floorspace. But this was a Soviet train, from the days when all things Soviet stood their ground. Soviet train tables do not fold.

I'd ordered our tickets on the Internet, well in advance of our river cruise from Moscow to St. Petersburg, from a Russian travel agent named Veronica.

I told Veronica that we wanted to travel to Tallinn, Estonia, from St. Petersburg, Russia, on the morning of June 14, 2008.

Veronica told me that she could not send the tickets to the US, but she would deliver them to our boat when we arrived in St. Petersburg.

I gave Veronica the name of the boat and our arrival date.

"We'll never see those tickets," Paul said.

"Have faith," I said.

Veronica sent the tickets to the boat on the appointed day. They were salmon-colored masterpieces with holograms and Cyrillic writing.

They were for the *night* train, not the morning.

Our visas were good until the 14th; we were leaving the night of the 14th. No big deal, I figured.

We'd planned to use St. Petersburg's excellent subway system to get to the station. But, the day before, Paul got his pocket picked in the subway.

It was slick. We tried to step into a car, but the man in front of Paul was raving drunk, obstructing traffic. At the same time, a woman pushed to get out, but we couldn't step aside because some jerk behind us kept jostling us.

At last, we were in. The doors were closing when Paul leapt out, yelling "My wallet!" I scrambled after him, to see him stomp on a man's foot and grab his jacket. "Give me my wallet," he yelled in the man's face.

People gawked; nobody moved.

I patted down the man's pockets, but there was nothing heavy in them.

"Over here," a voice said. We turned to see a hand drop something into the corner of the closed outer subway door. I gripped the thief's shirt as Paul dove for the wallet.

Paul flipped it open. His money was gone, but all his cards and IDs were there. I let go of the shirt and the man slipped into the crowd.

The wallet had held a few dollars and rubles, and one five-pound note he carried in case somebody kidnapped him and carted him off to England. Less than a hundred dollars in all. Annoying, but he didn't have to cancel his cards and IDs.

So we took a taxi to Vitebsk station.

So. There we were on the train, bags crammed beneath a cot and a staunch little Soviet table, clean sheets provided by the railway beneath us. We'd surrendered our passports to the middle-aged attendant with the tight uniform and bottle-blonde hair. We drowsed as the train chugged into the night.

Someone knocked briskly at the door, then threw it open. The attendant marched in with our passports. "You must go back to St.

Petersburg," she demanded. "Tonight. You get off train. At border. Go back." She thrust my passport under my nose. "See? Fourteen."

"What?" said Paul.

I explained she was saying that, when we crossed the border between Russia and Estonia, it would be June 15th.

Our visas said we'd leave the 14th. They would be expired by 2 1/2 hours.

"You go back tonight." Her voice was triumphant.

"Isn't there anything we can do to clear this up?" Paul asked, reaching for his wallet.

The attendant loomed above us, our passports clutched to her bosom, stolid as a Soviet table. "You leave train. Tonight."

She marched out of the compartment and slammed the door shut.

Paul and I stared at each other.

"Okay," I said. "When we get to the border, we love Russia." And we *had* loved it, for the most part, before this. "It's the best country in the world. The visa's my fault; I'm a dumb American. And your grandfather," I added, "was from Moscow, not Belarus."

"You're trying to tell me something."

"I'm thinking about that pickpocket in the subway. Your problem-solving techniques are sometimes less than subtle."

He snorted. "I should've kneed the bastard in the groin."

Fatigue eventually trumped anxiety, and we fell asleep.

Until 2 a.m.

The brisk knock. The wide-flung door. Ms Congeniality announced: "Half hour to border. Then you leave."

Slam.

We struggled upright. We pulled our shoes on. We arranged our bags.

I halted. "Stop," I said.

"Oh?"

"Let's wait," I said. "What if the guys at the border just want to get rid of us without a hassle? We won't know until we get there. We play Stupid Tourist, let them make the moves. What've we got to lose?"

He shrugged. Then he pulled his heart pills from his bag and set them on the table.

"Good move," I said. "If all else fails, we look old and pathetic."

A long half-hour passed, and we coasted up to the Russian border in the darkness, past men in overalls leaning on long-handled shovels in a coal trough. Rain pelted them, and the window above the Soviet table.

We ground to a stop at a stark barracks.

A knock. The door opened. A big black dog bounded in, snuffed around. A man followed. He barraged us with Russian questions.

"English," Paul said.

"*Tomas!*" the man bawled. He rushed off with his dog.

Tomas the Designated English Speaker was a broad, amiable man. He asked if we were smuggling drugs, plants, ancient icons. He smiled, a rare and charming thing in Russia.

Were we carrying more than $5,000 each?

"Hah," I said. "We're lucky we've got $50. My husband got his pocket picked on the subway yesterday."

"I think it was gypsies," Paul said.

Tomas the Designated English Speaker shook his head. "Gypsies are the worst criminals." He favored us again with his smile. "I hope your vacation goes more smoothly."

That's three of us, I thought, as he left, gently closing the door.

We waited.

We heard the whack of a passport stamper. *Whack, whack, whack*, up the corridor, to our door. Then…silence.

A jumble of Russian words that included *American*.

A cell-phone call. More Russian. *American*.

Knock, knock.

A small, starched man thundered in. "Stand," he ordered.

We stood.

He lifted both lower cots, dropped them, kicked at our bags.

"Sit," he ordered.

We sat.

He thundered out and slammed the door.

Silence. We held our breath.

Whack-whack. The knock; the door flung wide. A man set our passports on the Soviet table, backed out, slammed the door. Footsteps faded.

The train lurched. Our attendant ripped open the door without knocking. She was furious. "Estonian border," she snarled.

Slam.

The train chugged a few yards down the track and ground to a stop.

The Estonian guards knocked, waited a second, slid open our door. They asked questions in polite English, smiled, and didn't look for exit dates.

We were out of Russia.

[2008]

Back to the Earth?

Wildman Steve Brill held up a plant. "Hedge mustard," he announced. He tapped a finger on the side of a leaf—"Toothed, see? Ow—Don't bite. Hah—I'll bite YOU!"—and popped it into his mouth.

We thirty acolytes picked through the grass for the weed. I held up a leaf. The Wildman shook his head. Not hedge mustard.

"Here—have a bite," said a woman who'd gotten it right. I ate a leaf. It was inoffensively bitter, the texture a tad hairy. Not the plant I'd live on, if I were left to starve here in Brooklyn's Prospect Park.

Wildman Steve Brill is 60-ish, learned his trade largely from books, and looks like an unmade bed in his foraging clothes and frizzy greying beard. He has been stalking natural food in this most unnatural of cities for more than 25 years.

He was arrested, cuffed and Miranda-ed in 1986 for eating a dandelion leaf in Central Park. Which led to a publicity barrage, which led to dropped charges, which led to a few years as an official NYC naturalist tour guide. He met his future wife in 1998 on one of his tours. And, on this sunny Saturday, his patter was frequently upstaged by the exuberant expertise of the world's youngest naturalist, his five-year-old daughter Violet.

Brill has written a wild-food cookbook. He paints. He sculpts renditions of mushrooms in plastic clay. He can make his mouth a "Brill-o-phone" and play Taps. And, for a suggested donation of

$15 each, he leads popular foraging tours like ours several times a season through the city's greenspaces.

We were adults, except for the irrepressible Violet. We were male and female, young and old. We were white, Black, Japanese, Jamaican, and one French journalist who'd come from Washington D.C. to tape a radio report for *les gens* back home.

Brill pushed Princess Violet before him in a stroller, and we straggled after like rats drawn by the Pied Piper. We stopped to dig Field Garlic in the grass next to a walkway. "Make sure the leaves are round, not flat," the Wildman told us. "There's a flat-leaved look-alike that'll kill you."

A young woman grimaced at the oniony bunch in her hand. "I can't help wonder who or what might've peed on it."

We picked off the barfy-smelling flesh of the Ginko fruit—it's toxic, Brill told us—to get to the nuts. "Roast 'em for a half-hour at 300 degrees," he said. "They taste like a cross between peas and Limburger cheese."

We stalked fallen pods of the Kentucky Coffee Tree and opened them. Mine was moldy. Violet shook out smooth brown seeds and gave me one. Raw, they were toxic, but roasted and ground, they'd brew a caffeine-free coffee taste-alike. "There's nothing poisonous that looks like the Kentucky Coffee Tree," Brill said blithely.

Except for the Kentucky Coffee Tree itself, I thought as I turned the toxic seed in my hand.

The Wildman pulled down a branch of the Japanese Yew and picked bright orange berries for us. "Spit out the seed, or your heart will stop." Unless you were that old girlfriend who'd dumped him one Valentine's Day, he added, because she didn't have a heart.

We pulled dandelion leaves and dug burdock root and wild parsnip ("The roots are delicious, but the leaves are poisonous…").

Our four-hour forage was nearly over when one of our intrepid young guys leapt a rabbit-wire fence and dug up some Wild Carrots (the white roots of the young Queen-Anne's-Lace). "It should smell like carrots," the Wildman said, "unlike poison Hemlock, which looks the same, but smells like dead mouse."

Violet grabbed a root, sniffed, and stuffed it into her mouth. She chewed confidently.

When I got home, I dumped the contents of my plastic bags on the counter. I carefully cleaned the ginko nuts and stuck them in the oven. Then I assessed my greens.

Was that a poison parsnip leaf, or tasty goutweed? Was this spinachy Lambs' Quarter, or Jewelweed, something you rub on mosquito bites to make them stop itching?

That Field Garlic—were the leaves flattened because they were dry, or...were they always flat?

Sweating, I dumped the whole lot into the trash.

The Ginko nuts were delicious.

[2009]

There's No App
for That...

I pulled my new iPhone out of my pocket on the subway and scrolled to the icon for WordWeaver, a version of the game Boggle that had recently become my passion.

I glanced up and down the car. The crowd was sparse, and everybody seemed to be fooling with a cell phone, iPod or game device.

You have to concentrate to play WordWeaver. I couldn't. I felt uncomfortable. Creeped out.

I turned off the phone and stuck it back into my jean pocket. Then I removed my wallet from its accustomed home in my hip pocket and slipped it into my zipped front jacket pouch.

One can't be too careful.

My iPhone is new for the same reason that I couldn't play with it on the train.

Two days earlier, I'd boarded a crowded Q train in the middle of the day and propped myself in a niche next to the door. I pulled out my iPhone, scrolled to WordWeaver, and began yet another run for Level 10.

To get to Level 10 in WordWeaver, you must pile up found words, expose Bonus Coins, avoid little skull symbols and, as I said above, closet yourself in a Zone of Concentration. Everybody who rides a crowded subway creates a Zone; it's how you keep your privacy. You read your book or paper, bop to music, nap, or stare at the advertisements—Jet Blue, Budweiser, Jameson's Irish Whiskey, bilinqual ads for car-parking jobs or injury lawyers or English classes, the shiny face of Dr. Zizmore, who'll cure your zits, that poster warning you not to ride the train if you feel sick (too late?). You play computer games, chat with a companion, loll in an alcoholic stupor, or commune with otherworldly voices. Whatever you do, you do it apart, in your Zone.

I was in mine: Level 7 and rising.

The doors opened for the Beverly Road stop, and I leaned back to avoid the disembarking multitudes.

The Automated Voice of the Q had just warned us to "stand clear of the closing doors" when a hand darted over my screen and ripped the iPhone from my hand.

I gaped in disbelief. Then I sprang through the closing door after the fleeing form of a man in a dull-green nylon jacket. I screamed, *Stop him—he stole my phone.* I made a terrible ruckus and ran up the stairs.

He was out the turnstile and gone. I passed through, but there wasn't a trace.

That's probably not a bad thing. I was the dog that chases the car: had I caught him, the consequences could've been less than happy. Adrenaline is not a wise master.

The man in the ticket booth stuck his head out his door and I told him my tale of woe.

Would I like him to call the police?

No. What good would it do—I couldn't describe the thief as more than a tallish back in dull-green nylon. A fast back.

A man stood inside the turnstiles, on his way down to the trains. "You want to cancel your service?" he asked me.

And he helped me do so on his phone.

I regret that I was too shaken to get his name. All I know is that my guardian angel was an older dark-skinned man with greying hair and a Blackberry. And that he missed the next train on my behalf.

I owe him a great debt. Because of this stranger, the iPhone thief won't call some exotic location at my expense. Unless he has WiFi, he's not surfing the web.

He didn't get much. Mine was the oldest iPhone model. My "hot games" were WordWeaver and Scrabble. My music was Irish, folk, and one Feist album. He has my pictures and calendar. No credit card data, address—nothing of real interest to anybody but me.

I bought another phone the next day. IPhone lets you copy your phone content on your computer; I'd done that earlier in the month. So I just plugged the new phone in and got back everything I'd lost except the few bits I added after the last "sync." Sad to say, that does include a killer picture of a little old lady with her steel-grey hair in spikes, one of Ma's nursing home cronies who was celebrating "crazy hair day."

My new phone is faster, glossier, sexier.

It's also much more paranoid.

[2010]

The Sinus Special

My husband gave me a cold for Valentines Day, and I was in misery during the flight from Mumbai to Goa. My ears clogged; my sinuses filled with lead.

So shortly after we reached the plastic-fantastic Park Hyatt Goa beach resort, Paul dragged me to the hotel spa to see if there might be some Ayurvedic remedy to cure the common cold.

It turned out, according to the menu of services, that there was one: the Sinus Special. The description promised pressure-point massage on the shoulders and head, with aromatic oils applied on the nose, followed by massage around the sinuses. *Excellent for those with chronic sinusitis and colds*, the menu crowed.

I've been trying for years to get Paul to take a massage. He's the most Type A individual I know, a stress addict who, in our youth, gave up Transcendental Meditation because he was afraid he might lose his "edge." A man who has declared that athletic injuries are caused by warm-up stretching. If anybody could use a good soothing, it's Paul. So when he said he would submit himself to a back and upper-body massage if I agreed to the Sinus Special, I jumped on it.

The spa coordinator assigned each of us a tiny woman, and they led us to separate tables in the same room. We lay belly down, our faces ringed by those open padded headrests you find on massage tables, and our miniature massage therapists began working diligently on our backs.

Mine was very good. But my horrible Valentine's Day gift raised its ugly head, and my nose began to drip.

Someone had placed a shallow pottery bowl on the floor, beneath the head of the table. It was filled with water, and one big, beautiful yellow flower floated in it. It was an aesthetic device, something pretty for the customer to look at through the headrest.

My nose dripped on the flower.

Not just once. A regular, steady…*drip…drip…drip*.

Did my little therapist see it? Did she hear it? I swear that I could, even with my stuffed-up ears: a relentless tell-tale-heart *drip…drip…drip…*

What could I do? I was a prisoner in my headrest. *Drip…drip…* I consoled myself with the thought that at least it wasn't hitting the floor, where somebody might slip on it. *Drip…*

Then my therapist moved up from my back, up to my head. She stooped and removed the bowl with the flower. She pulled up a stool and sat down. I saw her little sandaled feet where the flower used to be.

Oh, god.

"Ib sorry," I said through the face ring. "I really hab to turd over."

"Okay," she said.

"I deed a Kleedix."

She handed me a tissue and helped me shift onto my back.

I could hear Paul sigh on his table. "That feels wonderful," he said.

I blew my nose, wiped it thoroughly, and settled back into the mood. My therapist tugged my scalp. She pressed around my eyes and massaged my face, and it was lovely. She thumped my head rhythmically with something wooden—which wasn't so lovely, but felt good when she stopped—and put warm, wet towels on my aching cheeks. *Ahhh.*

Then came the oil.

It turns out, because of a mistake in translation, the statement in the spa menu about the therapist putting oil on my nose wasn't strictly true. The oil was to go *in* my nose.

"I'll just drop this in and tell you to inhale," my therapist said.

Drop, left side. "Inhale."
I did.
Right side: *drop*. "Inhale."
I did.
SHAZAM—
I was back in the pool at Aunt Barb's, 25 years ago, all my nieces piled on top of me, none of them knowing that I wasn't playing as I fought to get up, to get out, to get free, that this was real, that my heart was staggering up my ribcage, that there was NO AIR; I was suffocating, choking, sinking, drowning—

I sprang up, sinuses seared with clove oil, *NO AIR*, drowning drowning *drowning—*

The little massage therapist's fingernails dug into my hand; her eyes went moon-wide. Paul vaulted off his table and grabbed my other hand. I was breathing; I knew I was. I was taking in air; my brain knew it—but my body was crawling off the table, panic red and fiery in my lungs, my head thrumming with it, watching myself in dread as the ride took me somewhere I absolutely did not want to go.

The spa's Ayurvedic doctor stepped into the room—he was about as old as my grandson—and he asked if I was all right, if he could do anything. He sent Paul's little therapist running out for lemongrass tea with honey—"It'll help your throat relax," he said—and I tried to find my voice, even as I gasped for the air that I knew was flowing in and out of my lungs without a hitch.

It took two cups of tea to slow me down, to let my reason overtake my terror. I apologized profusely; *I've never done this; this is crazy; I get uncomfortable in close places, yes, but I could always laugh about it—probably suffocated in a past life, ha, ha—and I never, ever knew this could happen, that it could unhinge me like this.*

The two therapists assured me it was nothing, everything was fine, but their eyes didn't believe it. Paul put his hand on my shoulder and shook his head. The baby Ayurvedic doctor explained the curative powers of warm liquids.

At last, they decided it was safe for me to get dressed.

"Well, at least your cold is better," Paul said, as he joined me for yet another tea at a table in the spa lounge.

But...even after all this, it wasn't.

[2007]

Driving the Road to Perdition

We were driving to the Park Slope Food Co-op when the guy in the black car-service car tried to cut us off.

There are in that single sentence four terms that I should define, for those of you who don't live in Brooklyn:

1) *Park Slope* is a once downscale neighborhood whose brownstone row houses, proximity to a park, and convenient subway lines have upscaled it. It's crammed with boutiques, wine bars, and young professionals with Golden Retrievers and Golden toddlers in Golden strollers. Which are usually pushed by nannies.

2) *The Park Slope Food Co-op*, founded in 1973, is a funky grocery store for members only, each of whom must work 2 3/4 hours every month for their nicely-priced organic rudebegas. Some of Park Slope's young professionals hire their nannies to work their shifts for them, an egregious no-no recently outed in the national media.

3) *A car-service car* is always black, and driven by a guy for whom English is the only obstacle that he can't run down. Car services are Brooklyn's non-metered taxis; you call rather than hail them, and haggle over the price for your trip.

4) *Cut off* is what car service drivers do. When you haggle, time is money in a whole different way than it is when you meter.

Anyway:

We were driving to the Park Slope Food Co-op when the guy in the black car-service car tried to cut us off. Paul was driving–

Paul always drives. He's a control freak, and my driving makes him grind his teeth because I leave space between myself and the car in front of me and let car-service cars cut me off. I'm not crazy about his driving, either. It's not that he's exactly a bad driver, but he tailgates, for one thing. It's irritating and dangerous, but since I don't grind my teeth, I ride. We don't have dental insurance.

Paul's driving was sketchy enough in Boston, where five-lane cowpaths segue to rotaries, and street signs are considered a fascist plot. He said he thought of driving as a game of strategy: "Don't look 'em in the eye," he told me more than once, as he ignored another hapless driver's bid to enter I-93 in a traffic jam.

Here in Brooklyn, drivers cannot live without their horns and their middle fingers. Stop for a siren-screaming ambulance; the guy behind you blasts the horn. Stop for a pedestrian in the cross walk; you get the horn and the finger. Stop in the wrong place; you get a horn, the finger, and a snarling Brooklynite with a tire iron.

So. Brooklyn driving. There are horns, homicidal maniacs, general chaos, bicyclists…and car-service cars.

Paul loves to drive in Brooklyn. Different game, different strategy.

Anyway:

When, on our way to the Park Slope Food Co-op, the guy in the black car-service car tried to cut us off, Paul kept going.

"Stop it," I said. "He's on my side–you're gonna get me killed."

He grinned. "Just sending him a little message."

"Send him a message when you're driving alone, so when he comes at you with a tire iron, it's not my issue."

A block later, the car-service driver tried it again–we were tailgating a school bus at the time–and again Paul shut the guy out.

"Stop it!" I glared at him. "*His* is bigger; live with it." And I didn't mean the black car (although that was, too).

Paul sighed and backed off. Two blocks later, we and the car-service car were side-by-side at the same intersection. Which illustrates another Brooklyn driving maxim: even when you gain time and ground, you don't.

When, at last, we parked on an obscure side street in The Slope–you can't park near the Food Co-op; you can't park near

anything in Park Slope because there are too many damned cars–
a man who'd parked ahead of us opened his car door right into the
path of a biker.

Bang.

The driver climbed out, slammed his door, and helped the biker up from the street.

"Look at my bike," the biker lamented. "It's f**ked up."

The driver turned and leapt onto the curb. "I get out, make
sure you're all right," he shouted over his shoulder, "I do that just
to *do* the *right thing*, and you give me attitude–" And he huffed
off, double-time, leaving the dazed biker to stand over his kinked
front wheel.

Another player; another strategic move in the game...

[2011]

The Rush; The Crush

Mexico City:

"Okay, *push!*"

Paul and I brace ourselves as the subway car screams to a stop and the doors jerk open. Bodies pour out of the car, a thousand clowns from a phone booth. We, thousands more clowns, charge against them to get in.

I reach the entrance; a woman crams ahead of me. The doors slide, scraping limbs, purses, butts. A man on our side shoves the woman's back so she is almost fully inside; the man beside her nudges his shoe a half-inch; a student sucks in his backpack; fingers flatten, stomachs draw, hips check. One; two; three; four tries, and the doors shudder together.

We, the Left-Behinds on the platform, inch back—a collective out-breath more than a movement—and the train pulls away.

And we stand, a rank impossibly deep and long, at the edge of the abyss, the long, empty steel rails below us whispering: *late, late, late.*

The subway in Mexico City is cheap—3 pesos, 24 cents, to ride anywhere in the city. An illiterate can read the stops: lines are color-coded and numbered; each stop is paired with a cartoon symbol. We are Line 1, Pink; our stop Juanacatlan, symbolized by a butterfly. The schema inside, on the car wall, shows a fat pink line with our butterfly, followed by a cricket (Chapultepec), followed by a bridge (Sevilla), followed by a bell (Insurgentes), etc. Little arrows with the colors of intersecting subway lines are marked above and below connecting station symbols. It's a great system.

If you can get on it.

The problem is, the greater metropolitan area of Mexico City is home to more than 21 million people. And all of them, from *niños* to *viejos*, are required by law to board a subway train between the hours of 8 to 9:30 a.m.

Or so it seems, when you're trying to force your way into a subway car at 8:30 in the morning.

We were in Tacubaya station (Tan line, an urn), trying to get to the Auditorio stop (Tan line, a cupola) to take a tour bus to Teotihuacan to an archeological dig. That bus would leave at 9, and we didn't yet have tickets.

Our landlord had told us about the tour bus. He had told us, *Walk to the taxi stand, ask them to take you to our National Auditorium, and catch the bus there*. But we saw the stop on the subway map. One station on the Pink line; a transfer to Tan, two stops. Simple. We had used this subway; we had tickets; we were experienced New York City strap-hangers. What could possibly go wrong?

We check our watches. 8:45. *Late, late, late.*

Mexico City was a complex of massive lakes more than 12,000 years ago, filled with prehistoric critters, from mastodons to saber-toothed tigers. The lakes shrank, and humanity came to the fore. The still-shifting earth below today's Mexico City is layered with pre-Spanish civilizations. There are ruins that date well before the birth of Christ, built by people whose names and origins have been lost, who came before the Aztec and Mayans—people whose compounds in places like Teotihuacan, on the hem of the city, are now being re-assembled like three-dimensional puzzles.

The Mexico City subway was begun in 1967, and unearthed artifacts—stone idols, tools, bones. There is a northerly station, Talisman (Blue line), whose symbol is a woolly mammoth figure because it has the bones of one on display. I took the train there a few days ago to see it.

I transferred from Pink to Blue at Candelaria station (duck), a huge interchange that is its own underground pueblo: bodegas, skin care shops, a McDonalds, medical clinic, pharmacy.

The Metro went above-ground. I watched the city pass below–businesses and houses, wealth and poverty, canals and desert–until the train pulled into Talisman (mammoth).

I had to exit the gates to find the mammoth. The area around the station might have once been handsome: two whitewashed entrances faced each other across a busy street. Each was flanked by a small plaza. In one, dirt and weeds straggled between white cobblestones, which surrounded a broken tree stump. Cracked stone benches slumped at the edges, empty.

On the other side of the street, the station's plaza was a sun-baked stretch of taxi stand with a lone food cart.

I found the mammoth inside this second entrance.

The display was a pit in the small and otherwise empty lobby. The pit was covered by a plastic bubble. The bubble was yellowed, streaked with dirt and caked with dust. I took a picture, but I can't recognize the skeleton it depicts.

A second train screams to a halt, as jammed with humanity as the first.

Paul inhales. "Ready?"

The doors shudder open. Once again, bodies slam into mine. I am forced back into Paul; the back-thrust overwhelms our surge, and we watch, impotent, as the doors close—open, close, open, close—beyond us.

The train lumbers away, a great red aquarium filled with bodies, heads, limbs, backpacks, all compressed, flattened like octopus suckers against the glass.

Again, the futile out-breath.

I am looking, now, directly down onto the tracks.

There is no one lying on the smooth steel, but it must happen. This craziness repeats itself every day, twice a day. How many people fall into the pit?

Yet…we are all still here. All still waiting. All still…*late, late, late.*

———

After my Mammoth sighting, I backtracked to Balderas station (Pink, cannon) to visit the crafts market there. Back on Blue; transfer to Pink at Candelaria (duck). Ten stops.

At each stop, vendors climbed aboard.

For a mere 10 pesos (80 cents), they announced, we could own: batteries, back-scratchers, magnetized plastic butterflies, souvenir pencils, scented markers, purses, newspapers, edibles, drinkables. And music. Men punched buttons on CD players and ear-rending music mixes filled the car. Ten pesos a disk. A snatch of one song; the next, the next. Each mix a genre: sixties folk; the Beatles; jazz; Mexican ballads; Italian ballads; salsa; old US hair rock.

Some people bought things. Music, especially.

I bought music on the street once in New York. The disk, I discovered later, was empty.

Perhaps vendors are more honest in Mexico City.

8:50: 10 minutes before our bus leaves from Auditorio (Tan, cupola), two stops away.

The train halts two feet to our left.

Doors creak open, bodies tumble out, thrust themselves at us. We charge on the diagonal. I grab the doorframe and throw myself inside against the human block. Paul crushes in behind me, compressing my ribs against someone's elbow.

My head is in a man's armpit as he grips the bar above; my back flattened against Paul. His arm is outside—crushed, released, crushed by the door—and he pushes harder, knocking the breath out of me. I apologize to a woman whose foot I stomp. She gives a knowing, tired smile.

I can move nothing; my arms are pinned to my side, my legs wedged against legs and low-held backpacks. I am grateful that it is morning and the man whose armpit covers my head has not spent eight hours hefting bricks.

The doors bang shut, open, shut, open—shut. The train jolts forward.

There will be no back-scratchers. No plastic butterflies. No music. There is no room for vending. There will be no thefts; there is no room for hands to steal into pockets.

Nothing can move. Nothing.
But we will make it to Auditorio (Tan, cupola) in time.
If we can get out.

[2013]

A Sea of Drowning Mermaids

11:30 a.m. Saturday: "Stand next to the fence," the coordinator tells Paul and me. "Someone will be by to give you instructions." Rain sifts down on my umbrella. Warm April rain, but it's June 20, the cusp of Summer. "At least it's warm," the girl next to us says. "This would be hellish if it was cold."

We are in Coney Island, waiting for the 2 p.m. start of the 2009 Mermaid Parade, leaning against a wooden fence that advertises Barnum and Bailey's Circus, dressed in brand-new canary yellow T-shirts with VOLUNTEER printed on the back. There are ten of us. We carry umbrellas; we wear see-through plastic ponchos. Paul wears shorts and a raincoat. We are Marching Marshals. I'm not sure what that means.

12:30: A trim blonde in a cowboy hat hands us hand-numbered signs on long metal poles. The guy next to me looks up at his sign, eight feet up against the drizzly sky. He cringes. "We could be hit by lightening."

The blonde tells us we'll stand along West 21st Street in sequence according to our number, and Mermaids with corresponding numbers will line up behind each of us. "You'll each have 25 Mermaids," she says. "Your job is to keep them moving."

1:00 p.m.: We're spaced along West 21st, leaning against the wall with our signs. Paul's and my numbers are in the three hundreds, in the rear, only three other Marching Marshals behind us. The rain has let up, but the sky is murky.

The lightning-phobic guy laments, "I wanted to see the parade. We can't see squat from back here." I sympathize fully. He brightens. "Hey, they'll put Harvey Keitel in the rear, right?" Keitel is this year's celebrity King Neptune. "Maybe we'll be close. I can take a picture."

The street teems with Mermaids in home-made tails and shell bras. Some aren't young. Some aren't women. Some wear only pasties on top. Some shouldn't.

1:15: Rain again. A marching band leans on our wall, chugging Budweiser. A tuba lies on the sidewalk, rain pittering its silver curves. A skinny woman in panties, two strategically-placed cotton balls, and gold body paint poses for pictures with a fat guy wearing only a jock strap. He jerks—"Oh!"—and pulls a cellphone out of the jock. He grins. "It's on Vibrate."

1:30: Rain pelts down. We stand in the flooding street, waiting for Mermaids to find us.

The band plays slurred New Orleans jazz. A nubile college girl in a sea-green, filmy, finned skirt shakes her butterfly-shaped pasties at a nerdy guy in a striped cap. Dirty old men click their cameras. Roller-derby girls swap war stories. Body paint runs; glitter falls; fins grow limp.

"I can't feel my hands," Paul says. "Look–my fingernails are blue."

1:50: Downpour. Gold Woman and Jockstrap Man rush by, thoroughly goosebumped. The co-ed in butterfly pasties dons a jacket. The band takes another Bud break. Nobody has claimed our sections, those behind, or the lightning-phobe's up ahead.

2 p.m.: Still no Mermaids back here.

2:15: Not one Mermaid. "They're not going to use us," the lightning-phobe exclaims. He sounds disgusted.

The pack of Mermaids up front jostles; we all start forward.

"They're making us march without Mermaids," Lightning Man wails.

An organizer approaches. Paul tells him, "Everybody's up front. We don't have Mermaids."

"Oh," the organizer says. "Well. You don't have to march."

Cool. We'll see the parade from the sidelines. "What a wasted day," Paul mumbles.

The organizer collects soggy signs. He hands Paul a board painted with the word "Spring," and me one that says "Winter." Other Marching Marshals get "Summer," "Autumn," and bamboo poles topped with flags. "Take these to the boardwalk for the Beach Ceremony," the organizer says.

No parade. No Harvey Keitel. We drag our burdens to the boardwalk. The rain eases; cold wind whips the flags.

The parade ends, for walkers and hand-pulled carts, on the boardwalk. All motorized vehicles—antique cars, trucks, floats—dropped off earlier, unseen by us. We lean on our props, waiting for the Beach Ceremony—whatever that is—as drunken Mermaids stagger by. Many faces, and bodies, are familiar. Jockstrap Man, still bare-assed, wears a jacket. The butterfly-pastied co-ed is draped over her nerd.

Harvey Keitel and his Mermaid Queen wife whisk by in a cart, so quickly that I can't snap a picture with my iPhone.

4:30: A coordinator shepherds us and our props from the boardwalk to the beach and lines us up. Four "gates"—red ribbons stretched between bamboo poles—lead down to the ocean like hurdles. Before, after and between them, we stand with our "Winter," "Spring," "Autumn" and "Summer" signs.

"You'll wait here twenty minutes," says the coordinator, "then they'll come and cut the ribbons."

"Who cuts the ribbons?" someone asks.

"Harvey Keitel."

It starts to drizzle.

5:15: Observers straggle down to watch us. I trade my "Winter" sign for a pole. The sign requires two hands, the pole only one; maybe I can take a picture with my free hand.

They sweep down abruptly: a bevy of Mermaids and Harvey Keitel. And the combined press corps of the entire free world.

Harvey clips the first ribbon with giant shears. I can't see him behind the hoards of photographers. The circus moves to my ribbon. My substitute holds up "Winter." I aim my iPhone and shoot.

The ribbon snaps. The mob advances to the third "gate," where Paul holds "Spring."

I glance at my iPhone: I've got it! A shot of Keitel's face, his glitter-covered trident, his wife, over the "Winter" sign. You can't tell he's cutting a ribbon, but...I've got it.

5:20: We march our signs and poles up the beach to the Coney Island Museum, where they'll be stored until next year. Paul looks chagrined.

"You finally got to do something useful." I say. "Aren't you glad we came?"

"Hah. When they hit my ribbon, the security guy ripped my sign out of my hands and held it up."

"Geez—what would he do that for?"

Paul snorts. "He wanted his picture taken with Harvey Keitel."

[2009]

Be Careful What You Wish For (Part 1)

I got my brilliant idea as we were strolling through the bohemian section of Udaipur at night.

Udaipur is a small city in Rajastan, in western India. It is famous for its miniature paintings. It is surrounded by hills and sits on a lake and the heart of town is whitewashed and touristy. But here, beyond the center, dogs roamed freely, picking at piles of garbage stuck in narrow ditches that skirted the street. The occasional cow wandered by, sacred and bony. Bored artists yawned behind counters in tawdry little storefronts.

We had stopped in three tiny shops to look at paintings. They were not as expert as the work downtown in the pricy craft shops, but there was an earnest charm to them. Everybody had miniatures of the usual Hindu gods on silk, old book pages, and plastic—flat little plates that were carved into curlicues at the edges. "Don't let anybody tell you it's camel bone," the artists warned—a stab at the downtown shops, whose owners insisted that their paintings were indeed painted on flat, curlicue-edged camel bone.

The artists trotted out painting after painting, and went to great pains to sell them to us; they were clearly disappointed when we told them we were just browsing. Not that I blamed them; customers weren't beating down their doors.

We entered the fourth shop, where the artist was already pulling out six-by-nines of Ganesh, the elephant god, and my brilliant idea struck. I told Paul I would ask for a picture of Kali, the dark goddess of time and death.

It was a perverse move: I knew I'd never find one, because nobody paints Kali. And I wouldn't feel so guilty about browsing for the fun of it.

"No, no. Tourists don't like her," the artist told me. "Tourists like Ganesh. Ganesh is wealth. You want Ganesh."

No, I told him. *It's Kali or nothing. My husband*—here, on cue, Paul shrugged and looked embarrassed—*has promised me a painting, and I'm looking for Kali. She's a strong woman; I like strong women.*

And so we worked our way from shop to shop. It was fun.

We entered the last shop on the street, and I once again did my Kali tapdance. The proprietor and main artist was a young man with piercing brown eyes and speckled hands (Paul asked, "Is that henna?" and the guy said, "No, it's a skin condition."). He nodded and said, "I have Kali."

He did. Just…not on him. The young artist, Nilesh Soni, dispatched his brother Manish—who introduced himself as Mickey—to their family house to find examples of his Kali paintings for us.

Mickey materialized in moments with three pictures on typing paper. He'd pulled a CD from his brother's art portfolio, stuck it in the family computer, and printed them out on their ink jet printer.

The wonders of technology.

I examined the three samples. Two showed the goddess dancing on a decapitated body, the severed head swinging from one of her eight hands by its hair. The other seven hands brandished various bloody weapons. Around her neck hung a necklace of skulls.

That's a strong woman.

The third picture omitted the dead body—Nelish said it was her last incarnation: so eager was she to be re-born, that she slaughtered her predecessor and danced triumphant on her chest—and featured a more stylized background of leaves and foliage. She still bore her severed head and assorted carving tools, and the skull necklace, the perfect foil to her skirt made of amputated human limbs. She had a nice smile.

"How much?" I asked.

Nilesh pulled out his big plastic calculator, and Paul bartered with him. And we bought it. On spec.

He couldn't paint it before we were due to leave India. And there was no way to send him a check; he had a computer, but that didn't mean he had a bank account that cashed checks for US dollars. So we paid him in advance.

And so, from the strength of a photocopy, we spent about 80 bucks for a yet-to-be-painted picture of a blue goddess with eight arms engaged in various simultaneous acts of bloody mayhem, who wears a serene smile and a necklace of skulls and a skirt made of severed arms. We paid in full and have no receipt, only a business card with two young men's names on it and these words, complete with rogue apostrophes: *Smart Art's—a feast for the eyes—manufacturer and wholesaler of all kind of traditional painting's on silk, paper, wood etc (specialist in portrait work).*

I'm sure our final price was more than fair; at Paul's urging, the kid threw in a small piece, made by one of his students, of a suave-looking Krishna with a concubine, painted on an old book page. But Nilesh said, "You got something from me—now I need something from you. Something from your country."

Paul and I looked at each other and shrugged. "We don't have anything on us that we can give you," I said. "What sort of thing do you want?"

"An MP3," the artist said.

"An MP3?" I glanced at his business card; there was an email address at the bottom. "I'm not sure I know quite how to send it to you, but I'll try," I said. "Who do you want an MP3 of?"

"Bob Marley."

"You like Bob Marley."

"I have never heard him. But they tell me he is good."

Will our trust in the proprietor of Smart Art's be rewarded? Will I get my bloodthirsty goddess, 6" by 9", painted on silk? Will I figure out how to download an MP3 and send it to India?

Stay tuned…

[2007]

No Sleep in Brooklyn

It was one of those things grandparents do, and we agreed to it—watching the boys for a couple days while their parents go to a wedding a few hours away.

"We'll get you tickets to a Broadway play," our daughter said. "I'm sure you'll need some time out alone when you're done." And she got us two primo tickets for tonight, Saturday night, to Avenue Q.

Kym and Reid live in a co-op apartment in Brooklyn. Actually, it's *our* co-op; we bought it from them last month, and they bought a house within walking distance. They're fixing up that house and living in the apartment until Paul retires in March and we move from the land of the 2007 National Champion Red Sox to that of the Yankees and Mets.

But now, we had come to stay in their bedroom and mind Grey (3 years old) and Beckett (1) on Thursday, Friday and part of Saturday.

Minding the kids during the day was easy. We packed them into the stroller (Grey) and the backpack (Beckett) and went to the local child-friendly coffee shop, to the zoo in Prospect Park (Grey loved the petting zoo. Beckett loved the loose gravel on the ground next to the stalls), to Grey's buddy's house, to the playground, even out to eat on Friday evening.

The problem is bedtime. The boys don't believe in it.

I will preface this with a disclaimer: Paul and I had three kids when we were in our 20s and early 30s. We were too young to theorize about bedtime; it was a matter of our own survival. The kids went to bed at 9 with stuffed animals and blankies. If they woke up at night, we gave them a sip of water or a pat on the back, let them know we were there, and left. Yes, we closed doors. Yes, we sometimes let them cry if there was nothing physically amiss. We had no monitors, white-noise or lullabye machines.

Disclaimer 2: our kids were all four years apart.

Disclaimer 3: We lived in an apartment when Kym was a baby, but our downstairs neighbor was somewhat deaf. When the boys came along, we lived in a house.

Kym and Reid are in their mid-thirties. Their boys are two years apart. They live in a co-op with a downstairs neighbor who is, to understate, not sympathetic.

The boys have phenomenal lungs and endurance. They feel that going to bed is not as much fun as the farm-animal petting zoo or loose gravel.

Their parents have negotiated a bedtime ritual: They read a story, turn on the white-noise machine in the bedroom both boys share, then lie down with them until they (the kids—although sometimes the parents as well) fall asleep.

Thursday night, we did that, and it worked well.

Friday night, however...

They fell asleep that day on the walk to the local restaurant where we were to eat dinner—Grey, in his stroller, and Beckett, on my back. They woke up to eat. By dessert they had both hit their second wind.

We returned to the apartment. I read to them. I turned on the white-noise machine in their shared bedroom. We each took a child and lay with them to put them to sleep.

But they'd slept earlier, and they took exception to repeating the folly.

We lay with them for a half hour, and each time we tiptoed out of the room, one or the other would rouse and cry.

Another 20 minutes: we tiptoed out of the room.

The only noise was white.

We poured ourselves some wine.

Five minutes later, Grey called: Where were we? He wanted us.

The kids were to go to a friend's birthday brunch on Saturday morning. I told Grey that if he wanted to go to Zoie's party tomorrow, he had best go to sleep.

Fuggedaboudit. We were supposed to be with him when he fell asleep.

I told him if he didn't sleep, he'd be too tired to go to Zoie's party. He was a big enough boy to go to sleep on his own.

Right.

The ceiling clattered down. Gods wept. The white noise turned black. Closet shadows stalked the room. It was the End of the World as We Know It, and he didn't feel fine. He sobbed; he wailed. He screamed.

I told him that if he woke his little brother, I was going to banish him to the bed in the guest room. A comfortable bed, I might add, and a room with no closets to harbor monsters.

He keened.

He woke his brother.

It was now 11; we'd been putting them to bed for two hours. I lifted Grey, carried him into the guest room, handed him a stuffed elephant, and told him that if he wanted to go to Zoie's the next day, he was going to sleep here. Now.

A moment later, silence. I went to check on him. He was asleep. He looked cozy and comfortable and—yes—happy to be there.

Meanwhile, Beckett was *not* happy. He sleeps on a mattress on the floor because he's a climber, and would be a regular in the ER if he had a crib with high sides. He scrambled out of his room and glared at us. He sobbed; he wailed. He screamed.

I led him back to bed. Gave him his pacifier. Rubbed his back. Left.

He reappeared, howling.

I took him back. Gave him his pacifier and a stuffed bear. Rubbed his back. Left.

He stomped into the hall. *WAAAAAA!*

It was now 11:30.

Kym had said we could just take the kids to bed, if all else failed. But we weren't in bed yet. We tried to get Beckett to sleep in our bed. *WAAAAAAAAAAA!!* It was our bodies he wanted, not our mattress.

We put him in his room and closed the door. *WAAAAAAAAAAAAAAAAA!!!* I thought about the downstairs neighbors, young and childless, who complained frequently and bitterly to Kym and Reid about the boys making noise after 7 p.m.

I thought it was too late to worry about them; they were surely drawing up hanging papers by now.

Paul and I opened Beckett's door. We went to bed and left him standing there in the hall, bawling.

And…he stopped.

I checked the clock. Midnight. I watched it for 15 minutes. Becket stood in the hallway, sucking on his pacifier to the low shush of the white noise machine.

Then Paul heard a tell-tale gut-rumble. "He's loaded his britches," he said.

I signed. I got up, walked over, and sniffed. Nothing.

But I'd noticed him.

WAAAAAAAAAAAAAAAAAAAAAAA!!!!

I put him in bed between us. He went to sleep immediately.

At 3 a.m., I awoke clinging to the edge of the bed. Beckett was upside-down, his head shoved into my hip, fast asleep.

I laid him back in his own bed.

Both boys slept peacefully. Paul snored. The white-noise machine shushed in the distance. I lay hyperalert, ears strained for the patter of determined feet.

At 8:30, Beckett pounced into our room, refreshed and cheerful, smelling like a loaded diaper. I dragged myself into the hallway, found a clean Pamper and baby wipes, wrestled him to the floor and set to work.

I had just put his clothes on him and set him back on his feet when a water bug—a four-hundred-pound Brooklyn cockroach—swaggered out of the kitchen and into my path.

I closed my eyes. Opened them. It was still there.

I pounded it senseless with the Pamper full of crap, picked it up with a baby wipe, and dropped diaper, wipe and bug into a trash bag.

We have just returned from Zoie's party. Grey is building a city with wooden blocks. Beckett is eating the playdough that came in his Birthday Gift Bag. Paul is dozing on the couch.

I am looking forward to Avenue Q tonight. I've wanted to see it for some time.

God, I hope I can stay awake.

[2007]

Pursued to the Full Extent of the Law

This morning, I got a letter from my insurance company. They are no longer insuring my car.

This would have been disturbing news if I hadn't sold the car three years ago.

The car that my insurance company no longer insures is a VW bug. Not a vintage Bug, engine in the back, no heat, the pick-up of a skateboard. A "new Bug," a piece of pop art molded from fiberglass to look like its predecessor, but more cheerful. I bought it new in 1999 and named it Helga.

Helga was smiley-face yellow. I drove her for two years, then lent her to our sons, who lived in New York City.

The car was paid for, registered and insured. All the boys had to do to keep Helga was to drive her carefully. No, that's not quite all: New York City cleans its streets on alternating days. So the boys had to move the car according to the posted weekly cleaning schedule to avoid its getting ticketed.

At first, Kramer kept Helga in Brooklyn. He was conscientious about re-parking her—or maybe he quietly paid her tickets and we were none the wiser.

He moved to Germany, and Kel brought the car to the East Village.

This was in the Fall of 2002. Tickets began arriving in the mail shortly thereafter. Not just parking tickets; *overdue* parking tickets. A New York City parking ticket, then, cost $35; an *overdue* ticket cost $45.

I received the fourth ticket in January, 2003. I brought Helga home and sold her to a local foreign motors dealership.

It is 2006.

Last month, I opened a plain business envelope to find a letter typed on flimsy stationary. It bore a Xeroxed letterhead with the name and address of a lawyer in Brooklyn. There was no signature.

The lawyer sought a settlement on behalf of a victim—call her Jane Jones—who had been injured in an accident in my 1999 VW Bug in Brooklyn, in January.

What??? Kel had *injured* someone in my car? *He hadn't told us?* In *January*, the very month I brought Helga home?

I re-read the date: January, 2006.

I laughed aloud. *Sorry, Kel.* I didn't own Helga in 2006. This letter was a mistake.

That night, I handed the letter to Paul.

He read it and didn't laugh.

"Come on," I said. "Look at that fake letterhead."

"Do you have proof of the sale?" he said. "A copy of the transferred title?"

"The title goes to the new owner. They don't give the seller a copy."

"A copy of the dealer's check?"

"It was a check. I cashed it. We spent it three years ago."

"This is a lawyer. A lawyer can take our house, drain our savings. All he needs is one 'T' that wasn't crossed."

"That letter's not even signed—talk about not 'crossing your 'T's.'" But I could feel the rock shift beneath my conviction.

This *was* a lawyer.

Paul called our insurance company the next day. The insurance guy told him to send him the letter; he would investigate.

Two weeks passed. The insurance guy called. He had phoned the Brooklyn lawyer. It seemed that Jane Jones had been a passenger in a car struck by my car, which had left the scene.

Helga? A hit-and-run? But...how was I linked with the accident?

The insurance guy didn't know.

Had somebody trawled for information with the NYPD and found Helga in the files for her long-paid parking violations? Was this the automotive equivalent of that grade-school boob-boo going on your "permanent record"?

The insurance guy didn't know.

He called back. It seemed Jane Jones had been traveling in the yellow Bug.

She was riding in a car and didn't know who owned it?

"I'm not quite sure what the problem was," the insurance guy said. "Sometimes lawyers throw out a net and see if they can pull in somebody with money. Say they prove you owned the car and lent it to the driver. Then you're liable for their client's injury."

I started to sweat. I knew damned well that I'd never injured Jane Jones. But I grew up Catholic; I still do guilt on cue.

The insurance guy called a week later. He'd received a copy of the accident report, and it seemed Jane Jones had actually been in a green pickup truck.

"Well, then. That proves it wasn't my car. If I did own the yellow Bug. Which I *didn't*," I added emphatically.

He called back the next day. He'd misread the report. The pickup truck was the vehicle that left the scene. Jane Jones had been in the 2000 yellow Bug.

"Mine was a *1999*," I said.

Papers rustled. "The report says it's 2000. You're sure yours was a 1999?"

Like I wouldn't know?

He read the model number. It wasn't mine.

"How can they connect my name with a model number that's not mine, on a car that's not the right year?"

The insurance guy didn't know.

He said the Brooklyn lawyer knew the name of the car's current owner. He also knew the name of the driver. Both men were "out of contact." Neither was insured. Jane Jones wasn't insured. "The lawyer probably told this Jane Jones person that he'd pursue her case to the full extent of the law," the insurance guy said. "He goes through the files, finds out you used to own the car. Finds out you were insured, so they look for a problem with the sale."

It's illegal to "waterboard" a lawyer. Even under the new rules. Pity.

A week passed. The insurance guy called again. His company would send a letter stating they had not insured the car at the time of the accident. They'd sent the same letter to the lawyer. A formality, he said. If the lawyer knows there's no insurance on my end, maybe he'll stop chasing me for a settlement.

And so, this morning I got my letter. I called the insurance guy. He said the lawyer had been in contact. "He sent me the same thing I would've had to dig for in order to support your case," he said. "A copy of the transferred title, legally signed over to your dealership."

So the case was closed?

"Well…no," said the insurance guy.

But the lawyer had proof of my non-ownership.

The insurance guy was as confused as I was.

I don't know whether to be relieved, or to buy a deadbolt. Is the lawyer an idiot? Is the case over? Is it even a case? Will I find a 300-pound goon at my door tomorrow, wielding a tire iron on behalf of Jane Jones?

On TV tonight, I saw an ad that told me to call Attorney Harold Sokolof if I had suffered injury in an auto accident. Attorney Sokolof, his doughy face righteous, arms crossed, toupee slightly askew, pledged to Pursue Your Case To The Full Extent Of The Law.

Previously, I'd found the ad funny.

I'm no longer laughing.

[2006]

Be Careful What You Wish For (Part II)

I'm standing in the post office waiting to claim a registered package and a guy behind me in line says, "I know you. You're that lady from Hospice—you came over when my mother was dying."

He hands me a pamphlet. On the front, it says: *God's Simple Plan of Salvation.*

I do remember him. He gave me one of these every time I visited his mother.

I sign for my package, wave my pamphlet in farewell at the guy, and carry my booty into the anteroom.

The package is a manila envelope with my address printed on the front in big block letters like you'd find in a ransom note. Stamps with tigers and flowers adorn the back at random. I feel something tube-ish inside.

I rip it open on the Formica counter, to find cloth wrapped around a length of PVC pipe. I unwind it. It is an original painting, 8 by 10 on silk, of the goddess Kali.

Her skin is dusty blue; her ample bare breasts not quite covered by a necklace of skulls; her skirt a whirl of severed arms. She has ten fully-attached arms of her own (She usually has eight, but we paid the artist well, so he threw in a couple extra). Nine elegant blue hands brandish carving tools; the tenth dangles a bodiless head by its hair. I hold up the painting: it's earnest and funky and perfect.

By now, the guy who recognized me passes through the anteroom. He stops and ogles the painting. His eyebrows fly up to his balding scalp.

I introduce the goddess Kali and tell him I have just returned from India, where I commissioned this picture from a young artist in Udaipur.

"They have thousands of gods there," the guy announces.

Bonk—there, on the Formica counter between us: One slab of scorn with a side of indignation.

Yes, they do. I explain that they're not necessarily a bunch of individual gods, so much as approachable manifestations of a general higher power. A way for people to connect with the divine up close and personal. Much as a Christian like himself might pray to Jesus rather than the scary guy with the white beard. Or like Catholics might ask St. Anthony to help find lost car keys.

The guy isn't listening. He's on message: this is his area of expertise, not mine. Bad things happen to people in India. They're poor; they sleep in the streets; they're covered with sores; they speak with funny accents—he's seen them on the History channel—all because they don't put their faith in the One True God. His voice is loud; customers sidle past us to the door.

The guy hands me another tract. I return it—*Thanks, got one; I'm good.* He gives me a pitying look and leaves me behind with the Mark of the Beast on my forehead and my obscene picture of Kali.

I re-wrap the goddess and her magnificent mayhem. I open the pamphlet: *Are you saved? Are you sure you will go to heaven when you die?*

All I have to do—it is *a Simple Plan*—is recognize that I'm a sinner and pray: *"For whosoever shall call upon the name of the Lord shall be saved." (Romans 10:13)*

I turn the pamphlet over. The fine print on the back: *"If you are saved through reading this tract, send us word that we may rejoice with you."* It gives an email address for a company in Monrovia, Indiana.

Food for thought.

Maybe I should take religion more seriously. God knows, so many people in this sinful world of ours do. They always have. Catholics took it seriously in medieval days, and sent crusades to kill Muslims for Jesus. Puritans took it so seriously that they turned from the Anglicans—who they felt didn't take it seriously enough—and fled the perversions of England for the inhospitable American shores. Where they killed off the natives, who were not serious about religion, and hanged a batch of witches they considered downright flippant, all in the name of the Lord.

The Catholics and the Protestants in Ireland took religion so seriously they nearly wiped each other out.

And European Christians got mega-serious on the Jews.

On Kali's home turf, Hindus and Muslims killed each other off with great seriousness in 1947, when the top part of India was split off and re-named Pakistan. In the early 90s, Hindus tore down an ancient Mosque in a holy Indian town because they suspected it was built on their god Ram's sacred birthplace. The next year, Muslims lobbed serious bombs at Hindus in Mumbai, retaliating in the name of Allah.

The Jews have been known to get serious on the Muslims. And vice versa.

Christians left a lot of Muslims seriously dead when Yugoslavia disintegrated.

And Muslims got serious about religion in 2001. Consider all the planning they put into killing godless New Yorkers to get right with Allah. It's enough to make a God-fearing, Christian Leader of the Free World muster his troops to take some serious hellfire-and-brimstone revenge on Muslims in return.

They weren't the same Muslims who'd started it?

Oops.

I might add that, in the aftermath of that serious exercise of religious freedom, Muslims are killing Muslims to show who's the most serious in the eyes of Allah.

I'm not serious about my religion because I don't have one. I grew up Catholic, but Faith drifted out of my grasp in Viet Nam.

Not that I haven't sought. I've meditated with Buddhists, sung with Baptists and chanted with Hindus. I've studied Navajo stories, Anasazi stories, Tlingit origin tales, Haitian Voodoo lore, legends of Celtic giants, Roman gods, Greek gods, Scandinavian gods. I read the *Watchtower* when neighbors bring it by. I've perused Hindu Vedas. I've read the Bible from cover to cover. Both testaments. I've read two interpretations of the Koran. I've read the Book of Mormon (I stole it from a Utah hotel room; I fully expect two young men in white shirts and ties to come looking for it).

So many books; so much serious religion. Anthropomorphic animals slaying unbelievers. Divine birds gobbling enemies. Gods raping mortals. People whacking people with holy zeal. Phalanxes of god-driven troopers, angels leading the charge: *Be brave! Be courageous! Be ruthless! Don't spare the rod, the staff, the spear, the sword, the cannon, the Kalashnikov, the Uzi, the M16; God is on our side! Onward, Christian soldiers! Allah will prevail! Kali will kick your ass!*

In the New Testament, Jesus preaches *Love thine enemy* and *Turn the other cheek.* The Romans take serious exception to this and string him up. Maybe that's why those Christians are so serious about scoring vengeance for Christ.

It's not Romans they're killing?

Oops.

This serious religion thing is complicated. I could use a little simplicity.

A simple plan.

I open my pamphlet again. *God's Simple Plan of Salvation.*

Cool.

I re-read the question: *Are you sure you will go to heaven when you die?*

Oh, dear.

I'm sure I don't want to. Considering all those serious folks who claim a piece of it, I'd prefer to go someplace more peaceful.

[2007]

Christmas Letter

Dear Amazon:

This concerns my recent order, which comprised a Yamaha keyboard, a folding piano stool, an electrical cord/AC converter, and a Yamaha PKBS1 X-style stand to hold the above keyboard.

I received all four items the week before Christmas. I opened the packing boxes to make sure I'd gotten the right stuff. I did not, however, open the inside product bags and boxes to count their components. Why make a mess?

I mean, what could possibly go wrong?

So here it is, Christmas Eve.

At 10 p.m., with the grandkids snoring peacefully in the guest room, I lay the above items out on my bedroom floor. The keyboard is lovely. The piano stool is simple to adjust and surprisingly sturdy. The cord/converter is...a cord/converter.

I open the box for the Yamaha PKBS1 X-style stand and slide the contraption out. And what to my wondering eyes should appear, but a stand totally devoid of hardware and instructions.

It's Christmas Eve, as I said. 10 p.m. Our five-year-old grandson will awake in roughly eight hours to delight in the surprises brought by Santa, in whom he still believes. Chief among these surprises—the star of the show, so to speak—will be the keyboard, *et al*, on which he will be able to take the lessons he's been begging for.

Sigh.

Okay, so you'd think, at 62, I'd be smart enough to check out every assembly-required gift early, and during business hours. Especially after last year, when I bought that little wooden kitchen sink from a local store and assembled it at midnight on Christmas Eve, only to find there was no hinge for the cupboard door. I rummaged frantically through my meager store of screws and nails, and I found—perhaps through the intervention of the Baby Jesus—a single stove bolt that fit and functioned, even though it wasn't the right part.

But there is no substitute in my screw collection—or in nature—for whatever is supposed to hold the legs and top rails onto the X in a Yamaha PKBS1 X-style keyboard stand.

I did find some black duct tape in a closet. Black—it matched the stand; that was good, right?

I carefully, methodically duct-taped the top rails and bottom legs on. I worked figure-eights, anchored with straight pieces, reinforced with tape-crafted struts. I worked, Dear Amazon; oh, how I worked.

It's after midnight. My stand looks like the sad, taped-up mess that it is, and it lists dangerously to the fore. Santa, if he saw it, would fire the elf who'd made it. The Baby Jesus Himself would weep.

I have cut the stand apart and jammed it back in its box, tape-goo and all. I've set the keyboard on our coffee table. Which is, of course, far too low to accommodate the nifty little piano bench.

I am most unhappy.

I do not wish to return the stand. Why should I pay to send it back? Why should I schlep it five blocks to the post office in the snow? Amazon screwed it up; why should I be responsible for your shortcomings?

I'm old; I'm tired. I'm a faithful, repeat customer.

What I *do* want is the hardware and instructions that go with the PKBS1 X-style stand. I want you to take them out of some other fool's box—that's what happened to *mine*, judging from the tape over the end that bypasses its tab-in-slot closure—and send them to me.

Please.

Then I want you to take that other fool's box and stick it in a forgotten corner of a far-distant warehouse basement so nobody will send it to the other fool, and put him through the misery I just went through.

You can do it. You play footsy with WalMart and Target. You sell maps and TVs and shoes and bathroom scales and, yes, piano keyboards. You can crush corner bookstores with a wave of your Business Plan. You're even able to convince the world that it needs Kindle. I believe in you. This is such a tiny request, a gnat in the ear of the great behemoth that is Amazon. How could you not grant it?

I eagerly await that little box with the hardware and instructions, while my grandson plays his keyboard on his kitchen table.

Thank you,
Susan O'Neill

[2009]

Dancing as Fast as We Can

Cory Booker wants me to join #waywire. He keeps trying to entice me by leading me to the site, where I'm told I'll be able to make my own alternative news feed because the traditional news organizations move in lockstep, serving up the same old hackneyed junk. With #waywire, I'll be able to see news from all manner of sources–especially YouTube–tailor what I receive to what I want to learn about, and pass it on as I wish.

Wow. It's nontraditional. It's outside the box. It's supported by the likes of Oprah, and Booker himself, one of its pioneers. It's the ideal news broker, the site claims, for today's young people.

I wonder: If I join, will #waywire discover that I'm 65 years old? Is there an #alarm for that? Will it send somebody to my house to rip my WiFi out of the wall—or wherever WiFi lurks— and arrest me for #ImpersonatingAYouth?

I don't, of course, *know* Cory Booker, the 43-year-old mayor of Newark, NJ, on a face-to-face basis. I know him through Twitter.

I set up my Twitter account early this year, when I came home from yet another workshop on publicizing one's book.

Most of these workshops are run by former publishing pros. Some are young; in the present media world, youth does not necessarily protect a publishing pro from waking one day to find he or she is former. Young former publishing pros become freelance gurus. They love to promote the use of Social Media to market your writing.

I've had a FaceBook account for years—well, for Internet Years, which is to real-time much like dog-lifespan-years are to human. Sad to say, it has not yet nudged my book onto the best-seller list.

But Twitter! Marketing for our age! Indispensable! The little marketing guru at the workshop raised his hands, a Priest of Publishing, acne aflame with The Spirit. You *must* be on *Twitter!* The ultimate Social Media *Tool* (Twitter, not the little marketing guru)!

So I set up my account. I am @oneill_susan. Catchy and original. The first tip-off that I'm #ImpersonatingAYouth.

The second tip-off would be that I had to read the directions.

Twitter is Intuitive for those whom evolution has favored with narrow thumbs fitted to virtual keyboards and the mental dexterity to condense all communication into 140 characters or fewer. To the natural-born Tweeter, *A Tale of Two Cities* would read: *Best/worst times: French revolt. Flawed man saves hero's head, loses own. Thwack! Mon Dieu. Madam DeFarge: Knitknit.* When you add the title, that's exactly 140 characters.

Those of us who grew up in the age of cryptographs on papyrus speak a different language. Virtual keyboards frustrate our fat, touch-typing fingers, and we cannot tell a story without florid, multisyllabic, mouth-watering adjectives. For us, mastering the Art of Twitter (#Twart?) can be tricky.

Luckily, there's a *Twitter 101* on the website. It not only told me what the hell "#" means, it gave me information on sending pictures or quotes or websites in a Tweet, suggested people I might want to "follow," and included handy tips on getting my own "following." *Re-Tweet, reply, react,* it proclaimed. I would begin as an isolated babe in the great Twittering woods, but once I started to *re-Tweet* other Tweeters' words of wisdom, *reply* and *react* to their messages, "followers" would flock to my own #Twitty postings. Which would, ultimately, give me an audience for my book marketing.

Fair enough.

———

I checked my Twitter stats today: I "follow" 20 Tweeters. These include other writers, one friend, the Park Slope Food Co-op, and a handful of famous people, including the young Mayor Booker—whose astounding Twitter output makes me wonder when he finds time for mayor-ing, never mind eating and sleeping. I've suspected that he is not a mere mortal since the day he rescued a constituent from a burning building.

I suspect he is a #Superhero.

Beyond sending out Tweets, Booker "follows" 61,000 Twitterers. Which supports my suspicions: who but a Superhero could read messages every day from 1,000 people, never mind 61,000?

And yet… He's holding a Twitter discussion on how New Jersey should kidnap the Statue of Liberty. He's offering his cell number to a man complaining that no cops come when thieves try to steal his car. He even told one guy who'd lost money to a city-owned vending machine to stop by the office and he'd reimburse him.

It's a bird…it's a plane…

If the number of Tweeters I "follow" is un-heroic (there were actually 21, but I "un-followed" President Obama because he kept begging me for money), my "following" is downright pathetic—11. That means 11 people can see what I Tweet. There were 16, until five of my "followers" offered me websites to connect with Hot Young Singles.

Eleven people to market my book to.

I'm so grateful to have them; how could I bear to spam them with publicity?

"Following" even 20 Tweeters means reading a lot of Tweets and pursuing a lot of links and pictures. It means a lot of *re-Tweeting, replying* and *reacting*, which generates even more Tweets, links and pictures. It's incredibly time-consuming.

Which brings me back to #waywire.

How can an individual with a Twitter following larger than mine but short of Booker's—the average wired-in Joe or Josephine, who balances Twitter, FaceBook, Linked-in, Insta-gram, a "traditional" virtual news outlet or two, the occasional crawl through YouTube to watch cats play piano, and a Tumblr blog, with a job, a family, a meal or two a day, a face-to-face social life and a couple hours of sleep per night, not to mention time spent publicizing his/her book—find time to engage in a brand-new Social Medium that will supply hours of exciting, non-traditional news-feeds?

Perhaps you need super-powers.

Or maybe you really, truly *do* need #Youth...

[2012]

The Worms Crawl Out

My worms have been committing suicide. Maybe they don't like the maggots. Or the New York Times.

It's my fault.

It all began early this summer, when I planted tomatoes in pots on the balcony.

I am no gardener. I don't enjoy it. But I love–*love*–tomatoes. Real tomatoes, not those styrofoam baseballs in the supermarkets. Tomatoes like my late father used to raise in his Indiana garden. From real tomato plants, like the ones I had to pick caterpillars off as a kid, which made me itchy and resentful.

If you want real tomatoes in New York City, you take out a mortgage and buy Heirlooms at the Union Square farmer's market. Or–if you have a balcony–you grow your own.

Last summer, I planted a spindly tomato vine in a big pot on my Brooklyn balcony. I weeded it, picked off dead leaves, dosed it with organic fertilizer, watered it obsessively.

In return for my uncharacteristic ardor, the plant gave me four tomatoes. The largest of which I could fit in my pocket (I didn't; you can't do that with real tomatoes).

They were delicious. But the ratio of labor to harvest could have been better.

This summer, I bought four plants.

———

I got the worms because I shopped for cars.

In August, our 10-year-old VW Bug was due for inspection, and it wasn't going to pass. The repair cost would be astronomical.

So. Car-shopping.

I learned that car manufacturers–Japanese, German, Korean and, yes, American–had, in the ten years since we'd bought a car, caught on that Americans like *big*. We like *power*. We don't need no stinking conservation.

Every car we test-drove got worse gas mileage than our old Bug. Even the new Bug. And the hybrids, while more "green," had grown too big for me to park–a major issue in Brooklyn.

We repaired our old Bug.

The car search made me ashamed of how wasteful I am in general.

I stocked up on über-efficient lightbulbs. I eschewed over-packaged produce. I started carrying cloth shopping bags.

I decided to compost kitchen scraps. After all, I had four tomato plants to feed.

I perused composting websites. I bought two five-gallon plastic buckets, poked holes in the sides, bottom and lid of one, set it on a block inside the second, unpunctured bucket to catch the drainage (Compost Tea, the websites called it), put the assembly out on the balcony, and dumped vegetable rinds, coffee grounds, leaves, shredded paper, dead plants and eggshells in it.

The stuff decomposed. Slowly. Fragrantly.

I hit the websites again. *Worms*, they declared. Worms would turn my garbage into compost in nothing flat.

I could buy them in Manhattan.

Macy's doesn't sell worms, but the Lower East Side Ecology Center does. The man on the phone told me I could order a half-pound of red worms for $11. I should pick them up on Friday at a booth in the Union Square farmer's market.

On Thursday, my worm dealer called. The critters would not be available until next week. The worms, he said, had Issues.

I pictured a Freudian preying mantis psychologist, a worm on a couch: *I'm blind*, the worm says. *I'm a hermaphrodite...I eat garbage...*

"What kind of Issues?" I asked the dealer.

"It's been a very hot summer," he said.

Ah. No hands: they couldn't open a hydrant.

The following Friday, I gave my dealer $11, and he gave me an old soymilk carton half-filled with dirt. The worms were in there, he said.

I tilted the carton. I couldn't see them, but I could hear them discussing their Issues.

I bore my cargo gingerly home on the Q train.

I upended the carton into the compost. There were, indeed, worms, and they set to work.

In a few days, I saw dirt where the garbage had once been.

The creatures multiplied. I don't know how worms Do It, but suddenly there were more worms than compost.

My 4-year-old grandson, Beckett, petted them. We discussed worm poop.

Then it rained. Water dripped through the holes in the lid of my makeshift composter, but not out the bottom. I opened the lid: fleeing worms crowded the rim of the container. In the catch-bucket below, worms floated in Compost Tea.

I scooped the fugitives back in, and plunged a knife through the bottom to make more drain slits.

The sun shined hard the next day. A vast field of crisp worm bodies steamed on the tarred balcony floor around my homemade composter. Inside the container, more worms lined up to escape. I scraped them back in. I shredded several pages of the New York Times and mixed them into the compost to dry it out. I made a waterproof over-lid from a flat aluminum-foil pan, and weighted it with my hand shovel.

More crispy corpses littered the battlefield the next day.

Beckett tried to pet them. We discussed dead worms.

Maggots appeared in the compost. They seemed to be eating garbage like the worms were. I suppose that's what folks mean when they say *It's All Good*.

The worm exodus has slowed–perhaps because there aren't many left. Now, I turn the compost and find a worm or two with every scoop of the blackening, lumpy, surprisingly un-stinky mass. I find a maggot or two. I find fruit flies and the odd ant.

It's All Good. I hope.

I empty the Compost Tea from the catch bucket every now and then on my tomato plants. The plants have thanked me with six tomatoes so far. They were small, but delicious. There are lots more, still green, on the branches.

I've found a nifty hi-tech composter on-line: you roll it on a base, and the garbage tumbles and aerates.

I'm thinking, maybe next year...

[2010]

No Questions Asked

I stood mired in WalMart amid televisions tuned to Dr. Phil. Hundreds of Dr. Phils. Thousands.

"Breathe," I told myself.

WalMart overwhelms me. I'm drowning in a great wave pool, buffeted by tsunamis of gleaming inventory—advancing, retreating, pulling me to buy. When I surface long enough to remember what I came for, when at last I grasp my particular pulsating silver siren delight, it turns to pressboard and veneer in my hands.

I never go to WalMart.

But I had flown in the night before, from Massachusetts to Indiana, to visit Ma, and if you want to buy a television in Indiana, you go to WalMart.

I held my breath, plunged my hand into a stack of boxes and grabbed a 20-inch flatscreen TV.

Gotcha.

Once the set and I were safely in my rented car, I mopped my brow and congratulated myself. I had survived. I had gotten a good deal. I would reward myself with a glass of wine tonight.

But first, I had to drive from Fort Wayne, where I was staying, to the tiny town of Avilla, 30 miles away, to deliver my prize to Ma.

Ma's got Alzheimers, but she's doing well in her new Assisted Living apartment. The Avilla facility came with cable access, and my sister Mo had told me that Ma's 14-inch TV, a relic from her and our late dad's house, was too low-tech to work with it. The new TV would be my housewarming gift.

I carried the box into Ma's spacious studio and gave her a hug. Ma has become a bit deaf, and her little old TV was blaring Dr. Phil's show.

She glanced at the box. "I don't want that thing. I get three Fort Wayne channels real clear here."

I wrestled the set from the box. "Trust me—you'll love it. It's bigger. And it's got closed captioning, so you won't have to play it so loud."

"What?"

"Closed captioning."

"*What?*"

"THOSE WORDS THAT MOVE ACROSS THE BOTTOM OF THE SCREEN," I shouted. "With this bigger TV, you could actually read them." I turned off her old TV; the quiet was instant, cottony. I put the little set in the closet and placed the flatscreen on the end table she used as a platform. "Watch it for a couple days," I said. "If you decide you don't want it, I'll take it back."

"You can't take something back just because I don't like it."

"You can take anything back to WalMart," I assured her, hoping I'd never have to find out if that was true. "No questions asked."

The facility handyman was off for the day, so the cleaning lady helped me connect the flatscreen to the cable box. Ma said, "I hate all those wires sticking out. If I had my dresser from the house, I could put it on that, and they wouldn't show."

She was referring to the house she no longer owned. This would segue into an argument over the way my sister Mo had parceled out Ma's furniture to family members. Ma had given full permission, but couldn't remember doing so.

I avoided the topic of the dresser; you can't win an argument with someone who has Alzheimers. The cleaning lady and I rearranged the cables. "They make special furniture to hide TV wires," I said.

"What?"

"ENTERTAINMENT CENTERS, Ma," I said. "You need an entertainment center for your new TV."

The cleaning lady and I tried to program the flatscreen, but we couldn't make it work. The cleaning lady left to go clean something. I pushed aside the cable box and plugged the flatscreen straight into the wall, where Ma's old set had been connected. Let the handyman hook it up tomorrow. Until then, she could watch her three stations on a nice big screen.

Ma frowned at Dr. Phil. "It's so dark."

I brightened the picture. The doctor's teeth gleamed like angel wings.

"I like my TV better."

I disconnected the flatscreen and reconnected her old set to the wall. I turned it on. She cranked it up past Deafening.

While we played her favorite card game, Spite & Malice, I entreated her over Dr. Phil's stentorian platitudes—when is the man *not* on TV?—to give the flatscreen another chance tomorrow, after the handyman got it connected. If she wasn't pleased, I promised, I'd return it to WalMart.

"They won't take it back just because of that."

"No questions asked," I assured her. "And I'll find you an entertainment center."

She threw the winning card on the table as Dr. Phil's audience applauded, vibrating the room. "Where would you find that?"

Where, indeed.

That evening, I sat in a Fort Wayne Pizzeria Uno and stared over my wineglass, across the parking lot, at WalMart.

Sooner or later, everybody learns to love me, the boxy building told me.

"Right," I said.

The waitress halted at my table. "What?" she said.

I stopped at WalMart the next morning. A different WalMart, closer to Ma's facility. In Indiana, every major parking lot has a WalMart.

I swam clench-throated through shoals of glittering inventory until I found an entertainment center. It was four feet long, ridiculously heavy, and came in a flat carton. The WalMart greeter and

I shoehorned it into the back seat of my rented car, then he went off for hernia repair.

I borrowed the Avilla facility's hand-truck and wheeled the carton down to Ma's apartment. Dr. Phil rumbled from her old TV. *"Voila!"* I said. "One entertainment center. Some assembly required."

The handyman arrived and set up the new TV. It still wouldn't work. It was connected to the cable box, but it still received only Fort Wayne's three channels. He promised he would call the facility's electronics wizard the next day. He programmed the closed captioning and left.

"The words move too fast," Ma said. I de-programmed the closed captioning.

I worked for three hours assembling the entertainment center, until I discovered I was missing a tiny wedge-shaped piece of plastic. It was the sole, vital connection between two beveled strips of veneered pressboard, and was not in the hermetically-sealed accessory bag.

I told Ma I had to drive back to WalMart for the piece.

She glanced up from a thundering Dr. Phil. She spoke.

"What?" I said.

"THAT TV IS TOO DARK."

At WalMart, the courtesy woman and I dragged another boxed entertainment center from the shelf. I ripped open its hermetically-sealed accessory bag and picked out its vital plastic wedge.

I sped ten miles back to Ma's place.

My sister Mo was there, arranging Ma's meds. Dr. Phil boomed from the new TV. Ma said, "That TV's been turning itself off."

Mo shrugged; she hadn't witnessed it. I tightened the cables.

Mo held the back of the entertainment center and I screwed it to the sides. Suddenly, the room fell silent.

The new TV had turned itself off.

"Must be the cable box," I said. I disconnected the box, reconnected the flatscreen directly to the wall, and turned it on. Dr. Phil roared back to life.

We were hanging the entertainment center's doors when the TV died again. "Hmm," I said. "It's not the box." I unplugged it and connected Ma's old set to the wall.

Ma pumped up the volume. "I told you I liked my TV better."

Two hours later, Mo and I finished assembling the entertainment center. It was big, bigger even than the disputed dresser Ma no longer owned. It would have been perfect to hide the new flatscreen's wires and cables, if the new flatscreen had worked. Instead, Ma's TV sat on top, a raving peanut on a vast plain of pressboard and veneer.

I gave her a quick hug and grabbed the dead flatscreen.

"They won't take it back," Ma said.

"WalMart takes anything back, no questions asked," Mo told her.

And that very night, they did.

I stuffed the receipt in my pocket, wrenched myself from the swirling, shining multiplicity of Dr. Phils, and dogpaddled out the door.

I staggered to Pizzeria Uno, where I ordered a glass of wine.

I stared out the window, over my wineglass, over the parking lot. At WalMart.

WalMart stared back at me. Triumphant. *Sooner or later—*

"WHAT?!" I said.

[2006]

Journey to the Underworld

Our guide played his flashlight beam over the Viet Cong underground surgery room's display case. I saw the glitter of clamps, handles aligned in ringed rows. Had I, thirty years ago, slipped gloved fingers into these very handles?

It was possible.

I was in Viet Nam, on a bike tour with my husband. We had met in Viet Nam in 1970, in the US Army's 12th Evacuation Hospital, Cu Chi. He worked as a transportation/evacuation officer; I was a nurse in the Operating Room.

The 12th Evac had sat on a mosquito-infested plot of land roughly 10 miles from here.

It was a busy place. We didn't know, back then, why one particular tract of woodland in the area gave us so many wounded. The US bombed that forest, dumped Agent Orange on it, sent in helicopters for close observation. Still, casualties streamed in.

Now we know that the enemy had surfaced from camouflaged tunnel entrances concealed among the trees. These were the infamous Cu Chi tunnels.

And here I was, thirty years later, seeing them for the first time.

The tunnels comprised a triple-decker maze of underground passages that, laid end to end, measured more than 150 miles. They stretched from the Cambodian border to Saigon. Some dated back to the French occupation, but most were built during the

American War. Viet Cong soldiers used them to transport and store armaments and supplies.

They, and civilians from the area, also lived in the tunnels. For years, while bombs blasted the forests above, an entire village worked, ate, slept, studied, worshipped, and died in this underworld.

That was then.

Now, the Cu Chi tunnels are a War-Land theme park.

We and our fellow bikers filed through the tunnel complex entrance, past the snack bar, a tiny zoo, a gift shop and a clutch of mannequins in jungle fatigues and camouflage ponchos. A banner above these proclaimed: "Please try to be a Cu Chi guerrilla—wear these uniforms and military equipment before entering the tunnels."

Our guide, a sallow young man in fatigues, led us to chairs in an open pavilion. He slotted a video into a VCR up front, beneath a picture of Ho Chi Minh, and wandered off to smoke.

The film was black and white, grainy: cheerful workers picked fruit and harvested latex, while a narrator spoke of "merciless American bombs determined to kill the peaceful village" of Cu Chi. "Like a crazy bunch of devils," she intoned, "they fired into everything"—property, people, "even statues of Buddha."

The film cut to the town's literal descent into the underworld. Soldiers and civilians dug with entrenching tools and hauled dirt out in baskets, extending their old French-era tunnels, carving out rooms.

I slapped at mosquitoes as children recited lessons in an excavated classroom and American bombers strafed a forest. VC generals hung medals on "American-Killer Heroes."

Our guide returned. He snapped off the VCR.

Questions?

I asked if there were tunnels near my old hospital compound. He pointed to a display map, and I saw a spidery sub-system beneath our base. What had they contained?

The guide didn't know.

But he did know a story about the hospital. His good friend's mother had lived in a nearby village during the American war. She often came to the 12th Evac seeking drugs for feigned illnesses, and brought what we gave her back to the tunnels.

Our guide led us to a clearing in the forest and challenged us to find a tunnel entrance. We swept the ground with fingers and moved leaves with feet. Nothing. The guide grinned, reached down into the pine needles, and pulled up a wooden trapdoor. We had walked over and around it, and around an air vent disguised as a waist-high anthill.

The trapdoor entrance was too small for us, so our guide led us to a larger square hole hung with a ladder. It was widened to twice its original size to accommodate Western butts.

He went down before us, brandishing a flashlight. We descended gingerly, conscious of clean clothes and aging knees, and followed him through a packed-clay passage. This, too, had been enlarged, but even at 5'3", I had to walk bent over.

We emerged in a high, wide space. A lightbulb illuminated two cots and walls covered with green plastic sheeting. A bedroom. It had once been lit by an oil lantern, which dangled from bamboo poles that reinforced the ceiling.

Another passage brought us to a spacious Council Chamber. Tree-sized beams held up the ceiling. The room was fitted with flags, banners, an easel-mounted map and a mannequin in a smartly-pressed officer's uniform. Mannequins in fatigues and civilian clothing sat around a long picnic table, painted eyes fastened on their ersatz commander. The effect was very creepy.

More passageways; more bedchambers. Then, the small operating room, with its glass instrument case.

At the 12th Evac, we had operated in an air-conditioned Quonset with adjustable tables and movable lights. We never lacked instruments or supplies.

In contrast, the tunnel's operating room was Spartan. Its table was, literally, a table—wooden, hard and flat. To adjust the height, they set it on blocks. Its camouflage curtain might have been a parachute. The lights were lanterns or flashlights. And those instruments: I could imagine the odd balky clamp disappearing from the trash at the12th Evac, to reappear in the hands of a VC surgeon.

All these rooms were in the topmost tunnel level. Our guide offered to take us lower; we slipped through a small door, and scrambled down into a tight, hot channel. Walking was impossible; we dropped to our hands and knees. Gone were those camouflaged vents; the stagnant air reeked of damp clay and mold.

I couldn't breathe. Ahead, Paul's bulk blocked the guide's light. The passage narrowed; my shoulders brushed the side walls. My hands grew slick with sweat and dirt.

I forced my trembling knees over the gritty floor.

The grade steepened; a faint, dusty tracing of light—

We squirmed out into a sunny thatched-roof kitchen. I gasped the sweet air that flowed in through spaces high in the walls.

Our guide sat us around a wooden table. He set out cups of lukewarm tea and a bowl of boiled manioc root, a nutritional staple for past tunnel dwellers. It was starchy and bland, potato-like.

At the gift shop, I bought a photo album by Vietnamese photographer Duong Thanh Phong.

The running commentary inside was propaganda, but the artful black and white pictures told the story: Vietnamese demonstrators protesting the American bombing; men recycling dud bombs into weapons; young girls sitting in a circle, rifles at their sides; kids huddled inside a bombed-out American tank. A man widening a passageway with a trowel; another reading in a tunnel's sunlit entrance.

A biker in our party marveled about the tunnel dwellers' tenacity. To live underground for months, years, in claustrophobia; to crawl through airless wormholes, to scavenge food and ammunition by night; to give birth, go to school, die without the warmth of the sun—this was dedication.

With their entrenching tools and re-wired dud bombs against our space-age Phantom jets, attack helicopters and defoliants, they were feisty underdogs—literally. If we'd seen them in a movie, we would have rooted for them.

It reminded me of an old joke: At breakfast, a kid asks his dad the difference between the words "involved" and "committed."

"See this egg?" the father says. "The hen was 'involved' in this meal."

He points to the bacon. "The pig," he says, "was 'committed.'"

[1999]

Startging the New Year Rightg

I was working on Christmas dinner, happy to leave the chaos of my grandkids' wall-to-wall new toys in the living room, where their grandfather watched TV. The kids themselves were torturing each other in one guest room, under the guise of "napping," and their mother, Kym, was napping for real in the other. Our sons and a couple of friends would arrive in an hour.

And so, in my kitchen, I enjoyed the eye of calm between the storm of Christmas morning and the late-afternoon tsunami of guests. I had sprinkled rosemary on the roast, my concession to the carnivores, and assembled a vegetarian broccoli pie.

The pie needed texture, I decided.

I would snip some sun-dried tomatoes into it.

I grabbed my kitchen scissors and a pack of tomatoes I'd squirreled away in the refrigerator entirely too long ago. I wouldn't soak them, because I wanted them as small, chewy bits of flavor in the creamier chopped broccoli and feta cheese.

I snipped at the dried tomatoes with the scissors. *Snip, snip.* As I said, they'd been around for some time; in fact, they were not so much dried as petrified. They flew into shards when I snipped, and I found myself holding them ever tighter as I worked.

Ever, ever tighter.

Which is how I came to snip the pad off my left index finger.

It was a neat little piece of tissue, about the size of a dime. From the very middle of the pad. Had I done it to all my fingers, no one could identify me if I robbed a bank.

I will say up front that it did *not* plop into the pie. It fell on the table.

I dropped the scissors and grabbed the piece and smashed it back on my finger, then squeezed hard with a paper towel as I began to bleed, big-time, into the sink. Once I stopped cursing, I called to Paul. "Bring me some bandaids. Gauze. Telfa, if we have it. Tape. Antibiotic ointment. I've cut myself."

I am the Queen of Understatement.

He ran in with gauze, telfa, tape, ointment and—god knows why—a tube of Preparation H. I held up my finger, and he turned white. I told him to cut me a piece of the telfa pad ("Do you have any scissors?" he asked. *Duh*), squirt a lot of ointment on it, and hand it over.

Together, we managed to keep ourselves from fainting or up-chucking while we got the bleeding under control and bandaged the finger.

"That looks horrible," he said. "Should we go to the ER?"

Yes, we should've. But.

I leaned against the sink, still pressing my now white-swathed finger. "This is New York," I said. "And it's Christmas. And the ER's at the VA."

We've been treated by the Brooklyn VA since Paul's COBRA lapsed in November. It gives phenomenal care. But holidays play havoc with the PTSD so many veterans suffer; I could imagine where I'd fall in the ER triage with a cut finger. By the time they got to me, it would've either died, or reattached itself on its own.

"You're probably right," Paul said.

I cleaned up the mess, and went back to food preparation. But not before I'd thrown out the sun-dried tomatoes.

When she got up from her nap, Kym was horrified to hear what I'd done to myself. "Why didn't you wake me up? Why didn't you tell me?"

"And you would've done what?"

My daughter is not a paragon of calm, and she knows it. She shrugged. "Um…panicked? Ran around screaming?"

Exactly.

It's December 28, three days since I discovered that kitchen scissors really can cut through everything, as advertised. I've raided the first aid section of the Walgreens on Avenue J and found some intriguing high-tech bandages: pads made mostly from water, gauze impregnated with an antibiotic that stays greasy so it won't stick, bandaids that meld with the skin and should not be removed until the wearer dies. Ribbon tape; cloth tape; rubber tape; tape made of magical spiderwebs and mermaid fins. Superglue, re-purposed and re-named Liquid Bandage.

I've changed my dressings twice. It looks like the thing might heal, but it certainly is ugly.

I'm typing with it right now. It doesn't hurt, but it's laborious; I have to go back and edit out stray g's and t's because the dressings catch on random keys.

This is how myh typing looks when I don'tg edifgt.

Helluva way to sgtartg a new year…

[2009]

If a Poster Lies on the Pavement in Times Square...

It was shortly after noon. A pleasantly sunny day, if not as warm as the last day of April should be in New York City.

Times Square was in bloom: the Naked Cowboy, tighty whities coy behind his guitar, strummed in front of the Recruiting Office's giant neon stars-and-stripes. Cops on horseback stood in file before Aeropostal, guarding a half-dressed model on the big monitor. Elmo hurled epithets at a tourist. Smurfette took a call on her cell. Two identical Woody-the-Cowboys competed for tips, as a Coke bottle competed with anthropomorphic M&Ms above them for facetime on block-long screens.

It was the ultimate commercial takeover of the heart of the city; the domination of *Blade Runner* via Disney fever dream.

The line to the polka-dotted van stretched back to the red stairs near the half-price ticket booth. "I'm gonna take mine home," the young man in front of me said. "Why not? I'm only here because of her." He nodded at his girlfriend.

She grinned. "I'm not taking mine anywhere. I want to see it *there*." She pointed at the plaza beyond the van, where two guys with buckets and brushes stepped over a checkerboard of faces.

I, too, looked forward to seeing my face walked on in Times Square—or, rather, a three-by-five-foot black-and-white poster of my face, one of hundreds pasted to the pavement as part of the InsideOut Project.

I started on my path to this line a few weeks before, when I watched a documentary at the Tribeca Film Festival titled *Inside Out: The People's Art Project*. It introduced me to the work of JR, a wiry, bearded 30-year-old street artist from France, whose trademark look features Wayfarers and a hat that might belong to your grandfather.

In 2011, JR won a TED prize, which gave him funding and a mandate to "Change the world."

JR had already begun changing various sectors of the world by mounting massive outdoor art exhibits. At 15, he claimed the rooftops of his native Paris with his graffiti. He later found a camera in the Metro, and took black and white photos of some of his fellow "outlaws." He was 21 when he enlarged and pasted these on the city's walls, humanizing some of the faces behind Paris's notorious 2005 riots.

His illegal face-pasting blossomed into a worldwide guerrilla movement. He and his volunteers plastered massive portraits of Jews and Palestinians next to each other on both sides of the wall that separated them. They collaborated to post the work of local artists in Berlin and Cuba. They celebrated women by pasting pictures of their faces, or enormous posters of their eyes, in countries where woman were decidedly uncelebrated.

And then came the call from TED.

You can watch the resulting TED talk at www.jr-art.net/jr. As summarized in the documentary, JR answered the call to "Change the World" with a challenge of his own: "I wish for you to stand up for what you care about by participating in a global art project, and together, we'll turn the world…Inside Out."

Since TED, JR's Project has included Haiti, Brazil, Tunisia—where the Arab Spring fostered such vigorous "free dialogue" over portrait placement that the volunteers feared for their safety—Rome, Thailand, Guyana, even Juarez, Mexico. The team has photographed and pasted in locales all over the US, including Oakland, CA; a North Dakota Indian reservation; Red Hook, Brooklyn, and the South Bronx.

And now…Times Square.

Our line moved forward, and I chatted with visitors from France, an Upper East Side matron, a guy from Queens, a Japanese tourist. And, of course, the young couple ahead, who lived in the Bronx.

My turn came. I signed disclaimers on an iPad, and a volunteer led me to the back of the polka-dotted van. Inside was a tiny photo booth, where I took a stool opposite a camera imbedded in the wall. The volunteer tapped the mirror; I had six seconds to pull an appropriate face. I recoiled dramatically from the feet destined to troop across my likeness, and the shutter snapped.

I stepped out. My portrait printed and rolled from a slot in the side of the van. The volunteer handed it to me and used my phone to take my picture with it. She rolled it up and told me that the team had a backlog of pictures because it had rained yesterday and they couldn't paste (When it rains, they remove the old posters from the pavement because they become dangerously slippery). So they'd be pasting yesterday's posters this afternoon, and ours later this evening or tomorrow morning.

"How long do the posters stay down?" I asked.

"They're temporary by design," she said. "But mine stayed put for five days—the weather was dry. Come back tomorrow; we'll have you pasted by then."

I was disappointed that, unlike the subjects in JR's movie, I wouldn't be doing my own pasting. I was even more disappointed that I'd have to wait until tomorrow to see my poster on the ground.

Sure, it was temporary, and nobody would recognize me anyway, and my likeness was far from gorgeous. But still…

Whoa.

What's with the ego? I asked myself. There is no inherent "meaning" in the Times Square project. It doesn't highlight the resilience of the Haitians, or celebrate victimized women, or reveal the faces of persecuted LGTB Russians, or remind Equadorians that they have Indian minorities.

Times Square is just…faces.

My picture would be pasted down among hundreds, maybe

thousands, then washed away by rain or worn away by feet, or scraped up by JR's volunteers to avoid injury lawsuits. What was the big deal if I couldn't paste it down myself? And why did it matter that I wouldn't see it on the sidewalk the day it was taken?

I was lucky, really: This was Tuesday; we were leaving Thursday for Maine to see Paul's mom, and I'd have a day to take a picture of myself in the square. I could show it to her; Ev would enjoy that. I could post it on Facebook and Twitter.

I returned Wednesday afternoon, my phone set to Camera.

My picture wasn't there.

People who'd just had their pictures taken were handing their posters to the pasting guys. A few of the subjects seemed to be helping with the glue and brushes.

I asked one of the volunteers where yesterday's pictures were.

She shrugged. "We're alternating some of them with the new ones."

I looked for the older posters. I didn't see a pile, a box, even a rolled poster—just people handing over their new likenesses, which went straight to the cement.

Mine would get pasted while I was gone, and I'd miss it. I would have no photo for Ev, or Facebook or Twitter.

I suppressed the urge to beg the volunteer to find my poster.

Patience, I told myself. It was probably waiting its turn in the polka-dotted truck.

Or maybe, an evil voice whispered in my brain, *it's in the trash.*

We left for Maine the next day. We returned on Monday. It hadn't rained in New York; perhaps my poster had survived the weekend. I took the Q train Tuesday morning to Times Square.

I passed Woody and Woody. I dodged Elmo, edged around two well-endowed, guitar-toting women in skimpy undies—Naked Cowgirls??—and slipped through knots of tourists posing with a bored Smurfette.

The polka-dotted van was busy. The pavement in front of the red stairs was covered with faces, some tattered and some brand-new. A tall, wide building behind the half-price ticket booth was pasted from top to bottom with posters.

I walked every inch of the plaza. I was not there.

I examined the building. I was not there.

Was my face walked on by tourists last weekend? Was it hidden beneath a new poster? Was it pasted at all?

If a face lies on the pavement in Times Square and nobody recognizes it, does it make a difference?

I stood back and surveyed the square.

It looked...stunning. Dizzying.

Grand.

Here was the ultimate human takeover of the heart of the city; a glorious domination of *faces, faces, faces*.

My heart swelled.

I didn't recognize a single one. But I had represented; I had been a tiny part of this in some impermanent way.

That, I realized, was a very cool thing.

[2013]

Heineken: What It's All About

I have here a six-inch-high buffed-aluminum fake Heineken bottle.

The label is stamped into the metal. An elegant silver fake label. "Heineken" at the top, small white letters on the traditional black scroll; perky red star above, little green vine beneath. Three inches of whitespace (silverspace?), then the words "premium quality" in miniature san-serif caps.

The fake bottle splits into lengthwise halves, to reveal a rectangular stainless-steel bottle opener nested in black matte plastic. It's a gift from Heineken of Amsterdam.

It is a golden box for a cardboard tiara, perfectly suited to the Heineken Brewery tour, which is all about marketing.

Touring Heineken was not my first choice of activities in Amsterdam. My first choice was the cake bakery across the street. Black Forest torte with whipped cream; thick cappuccino. Purple- and yellow-iced cakes scattered about for decoration (The icing was real, or the ant climbing the swan torte in the window was delusional).

But boys will be boys: Paul saw the brewery the moment we waddled out of the bakery. So we plunked down 11 Euros each for The Heineken Experience.

Eleven Euros is a lot of money for a brewery tour. And this

was not a real brewery. The real Heineken brewery is somewhere between Amsterdam and Rotterdam This is the former brewery and current Heineken Experience Welcome Center.

In fairness, the fee included four plastic tokens. Three would buy us drinks at "pubs" during the tour. The fourth granted us a gift at the end.

I told the man at the desk that I don't like beer. *Keep the tokens; give me a discount.*

He couldn't do that—but I could use my tokens for Cokes. *I don't like Coke, either.*

He shrugged and handed me my tokens.

The first stop on the tour was the Heineken history room.

The brewery was built by Gerard Heineken in the 1880s.

Freddy Heineken, Gerard's grandson, studied beer salesmanship in the 1940s in the US. He returned to declare his office Heineken's first Advertising Department.

There was a TV monitor devoted to Freddy. Punch the button: a dour black-and-white Freddy Heineken explains that beer is a Happy Drink, and beer advertising should highlight Good Times. *Punch*: Freddy explains that he slanted the e's in Heineken to make them cheerful. He frowns as he speaks of his "smiling e."

A wall in the room was covered with old Heineken ads. One featured hip young Black drinkers. The French caption: *Heineken—c'est la bière de l'élite.*

Two ads featured three-panel pictures, titled: *Heineken refreshes the parts other beers cannot reach.* The first showed Star Trek's Mr. Spock, looking dubious, then raising a glass of Heineken, then brandishing the empty glass. A cartoon balloon above this image says, *Logical.*

The second triptich pictures a fat, frowsy woman in a Queen Mum shirtdress and little hat, beerless. Next, she has a full mug. Finally, her mug is empty and she wears a paper bag over her head, enjoying some refreshed part other beers cannot reach.

We walked upstairs, into a fake brewing room, where we saw lots of copper, and—through a window—a stable full of Clydesdales. Exchange students from Budweiser?

The first "pub" was a long wooden bar where bartenders filled and distributed glasses of Heineken assembly-line style.

I took a Heineken.

Heineken had once been a big deal in US bars. It was Imported, and therefore exotic. You bought it to impress somebody. Freddy Heineken had sold his image masterfully.

As for the beer itself... I don't like beer. For me, it might as well be Budweiser.

Just beyond the "pub" was a stage where people stood in front of a bluescreen and sang along with a karaoke monitor. A video camera recorded this, and you could send it to an email address.

Paul and I took a turn, chewed on the Dutch words that flowed across the screen—something about tulips—and sent the video to his workplace.

Up more stairs, to "ride the Heineken wagon." A man gated four of us into a fake wagon bench. The seat bucked up and down as we watched a video of Clydesdales pulling us through the streets of Amsterdam. Happy townspeople crawled out of the city's famed coffee houses and cheered as we passed.

The video brought us into a barn. The seat stopped bucking. We left.

Up more stairs.

And here lay Mecca.

My BA is in Journalism/Advertising. I loved ad classes. Smoke in boxes; test audiences with wires stuck to their eyelids; clever puns. What's not to love about advertising?

This room was filled with lounge chairs, each fitted with an overhead monitor that played Heineken TV ads.

I crawled into a chair and pulled the monitor close.

The ads started with 1955 and ended in present day. You watched the stream by clicking a button on the arm of the chair. Bored? *Click*—skip a month, a year, a decade.

I knew this clicking was not an idle activity for Heineken. The armchair button was computerized so they could determine which commercials merited thirty seconds of my attention, and which I dismissed before the last frame. It was an advertiser's wet dream: no need to hire a starving actor to collar shoppers in a mall and beg them to critique ads for two bucks. Here, hundreds of eager volunteers paid for the privilege.

After a half-hour, Paul tapped me on the shoulder. I reluctantly crawled out of my sanctuary of singing bottles, beer-guzzling astronauts and parties, parties, parties.

It was, once again, "pub" time.

The bartender had a terrific handlebar mustache. He zipped full glasses of Heineken left and right, and poured me a glass of water without missing a beer-beat.

A skinny back-packer asked if I had any spare tokens. He looked like he'd been using Heineken as a major food group. I gave him what I had left. Paul did, too.

He's probably still at the "pub."

We cashed in our "gift" chips on our way out. I am looking at my gift now: my aluminum fake Heineken bottle. It's too modern for our mantelpiece, too big to mount amid the totems atop my computer, too bulky for a paperweight. Too light for a bookend; too small to rig as a lamp. Hopelessly unsuited as a vase. I can't employ it as a gift box, because the only thing that will fit inside is the bottle opener, and what kind of gift is a bottle opener?

I'd toss it in the trash, but…it's too pretty.

My fake Heineken bottle will outlive me. Perhaps, like the less classy cockroach, it will outlive nuclear war and the next ice age. Eons hence, some advanced life form will dig in earth's ashes for clues to our poor follies.

They will find my fake Heineken bottle.

They will be dazzled by its style, and puzzle over its function.

They will conclude that it is an idol of worship.

Mr. Spock would say: *Logical.*

[2007]

Two Dog Night

I picked my way down the aisle of the Greyhound, avoiding that guy hacking like Ratzo Rizzo, and discovered two empty seats near the back. Could it be that—in spite of the Easter rush, in spite of the packed bus from Florence, SC, in spite of the 2 1/2-hour delay in Fayetteville, in spite of the run of lousy luck that had brought me here in the first place—I would be able to stretch out and grab some Z's between here and Richmond?

Pull away, Bus, I prayed. *Now.*

The Largest Man in the World lurched up the aisle. Eight feet, 600 pounds. Taco Bell bag clutched to his chest, wrapped in the stench of tired chimichangas.

He halted at my seat. Hunkered in.

There is no god.

I had just finished an author gig at Francis Marion University in Florence. The students were courteous and intelligent; my hosts, English professor Jon Tuttle and his lovely wife Cheryl, were great fun. There was sunshine, laughter; there were insightful questions. There was even a paycheck.

It was good.

Then I tried to get home.

I'd bought my tickets from Spirit Air two months earlier on line. I had never flown Spirit, but it flew non-stop to Myrtle Beach, an hour from Florence. My tickets were for April 1, returning April 3.

The flight to Myrtle Beach was uneventful.

However, on April 3—the day before Easter—I arrived at the Myrtle Beach airport to discover that my return flight was canceled. Explanations were vague and unsatisfactory, and spirits in the Spirit ticket line were not high.

There were many of us. We inched to the counter, one by one, where the clerk told us she could get us to NYC late tomorrow, Easter night. Spirit could not book or reimburse for hotels.

When my turn came, she shook her head at my ticket information. "This says *May* third. There's nothing I can do."

I'm a night owl. I made my reservations at 2 a.m. I routinely make reservations at 2 a.m. Done it for years; never screwed up. But the Spirit Air website was tricky; it not only flipped the month on me, but because I didn't un-check a box, it sold me "optional" cancellation insurance.

Unfortunately, Spirit's cancellation for my *May 3* flight had not happened. Not yet, at least.

I sat on the airport floor—there were no seats—and called Amtrak. Their only train before Easter was full.

So I called Greyhound.

Last month, I traveled Greyhound for the first time since the '60s. Paul and I were on a multi-city vacation; we booked a bus for one short leg to avoid steep rental-car drop-off fees. That bus had left five hours late, and lost more time as it rode. I had reason to fear the Dog.

But what could I do? Renting a car would be expensive and laborious. If I got a flight—impossible, since Spirit was serving *April 3* passengers first—I would miss Easter dinner with the family.

Greyhound's phone guy said the bus would leave Florence at 7:30 p.m. and arrive in NYC at 10 a.m on Easter. I was to come an hour early.

Jon and Cheryl Tuttle gamely ferried me back to Florence to catch my bus.

I showed up, as ordered, an hour early. The station was locked. "They open it at 7," a fellow rider informed me.

A kid wandered up with a tray of saran-wrapped brownies. "Best Brownies in the World," he announced. "One dollar each."

"How do you know they're the best in the world?" I asked.

"I tasted 'em." Michelle had made them, he said, and she was the Best Baker in the World.

A paint-peeling old Chevy ground through the lot, driven by a madwoman in silver cat's-eye shades. She rolled down the window, blasting us with Michael Jackson, and waved. Michelle.

I bought a brownie.

The Greyhound agent unlocked the door at 7. At 7:30, the bus pulled in. All of us managed to get aboard, even those who had not gotten on the earlier bus because Greyhound sells more tickets than they have seats.

The first leg of the trip, from Florence to Fayetteville, ran on time. I sat beside an attractive, smart young woman. She worked in a fast-food joint, and it was wearing on her. Didn't know what she wanted to be; didn't have money to be it. Was on her way to sign up for the Army. "My sister's already in the Air Force," she said, "but they met their quota for new recruits."

I offered her the Best Brownie in the World. She said she wasn't hungry.

We were to change buses in Fayetteville, but our new bus was being fixed because it couldn't go over 55 miles per hour. So we all stood in line. One hour passed. Two. The young man ahead of me had three bus-changes ahead to get to Pittsburgh, where he was a junior in college. "I'll never make my connections," he lamented.

This would be his last college semester. He drew out a benefits sheet from his Army recruiter. He worked three part-time jobs, but he still had student loan debts of $65,000. The Army would cover it all for him if he joined for three years and waived some of his GI Bill benefits. "I don't want to leave the US," he said. "Especially to go to Iraq or Afghanistan. But this debt is killing me; I don't know how else I'll ever pay it off."

I offered him the Best Brownie in the World. He took it eagerly.

At last, after two and one-half hours of sitting on our bags, we were called to our—repaired, we hoped—bus.

I found my seat. That's when the Largest Man in the World arrived, bearing Taco Bell.

It is not easy to sleep when you share a seat with the Largest Man in the World. Especially when he snores. A *snork-snork-snork* that halts abruptly, leaving you panicked that he's died–*My god, I'll be trapped here forever*—then, *snork-snork-snork.*

And then there was the Taco Bell issue. I sure you get my… er…drift.

Somehow, in time, I managed to doze. And woke, squashed and cranky, as we pulled into Richmond.

The bus disappeared. To be repaired. *Re*-repaired: same problem. We were hours late already. Our 45-minute rest stop stretched to an hour, then two.

We reboarded at last. The Largest Man in the World beckoned me to the seat beside him. "Nothing personal," I said, and walked on by.

I took a seat next to another, smaller, man and I fell asleep.

I woke at 9 a.m.; the sun beamed on the Washington Monument, the Capitol dome, the bikepaths of DC. The driver revised our New York ETA from 10 a.m. to 2 p.m.

Next: Baltimore.

Up front, Ratzo *hacked*. The Largest Man in the World belched. The man behind me phone-talked three women—his kids' mom, the girlfriend who was picking him up in NYC, and somebody called Sugar, as in "Oh, *Sugar*, you know I wanna, but I'm stuck here in DC for a week with my old friend Lionel, remember Lionel?" Little kids stirred from a night's uneasy sleep. Michael Jackson leaked from the earphones of the woman in front of me.

And the Dog lumbered on, on, on.

[2010]

Starving in the Fort

I'd flown into Fort Wayne via Chicago, and I was starving. I'd gotten up too early to eat breakfast, and I'd flown American Airlines.

American Airlines not only charges hefty fees for each checked bag, it also charges for snacks. You want your peanuts, you pay for your peanuts. I didn't have any money left after paying for my bag, so…no peanuts.

So when I hit the city of my birth, I was looking forward to the two treats for which Fort Wayne International Airport is famous: the Cookie Lady, and De Brand Chocolate.

The Cookie Lady is cheerful and grandmotherly, straight out of Central Casting. She toddles through the entrance hall with a basket of free cookies, each hermetically sealed in its own little plastic baggie. They're made at a cookie factory across the street. Yes, a cookie *factory*, not a cookie bakery; this is Indiana. Soft sugar cookies, hot off the assembly line, bland and sweet.

Yum.

I reached the terminal entrance hall and glanced up and down, from the ticket counters to the baggage carousels—which is, in Fort Wayne International, roughly ten feet—and…

No Cookie Lady.

Gone.

Somebody "downsized" the Cookie Lady??

But the De Brand Chocolate counter was there.

In my youth, Fort Wayne was home to the likes of International Harvester, Magnavox, General Electric, and a plethora of factories that supported Detroit, like Goodrich Tire, where my father worked. Now, most of those conglomerates have decentralized, leaving the Fort with their crumbs (Goodrich is now one of several plants owned by Michelin), or closed down, or moved south or to China. There is industry here—quite a bit of it, unlike in Elkhart or South Bend—but mostly smaller businesses or the aforementioned pieces of mega-corporations.

But: the city hosts two popular companies of its very own.

One is Vera Bradley, which makes those flowery quilted bags prized by little old ladies all over the planet.

A couple of visits ago, I hit the Vera Bradley shop in the city's newest mall to support the Old Home team. I discovered a cheery red bandana-print backpack, the perfect size to carry a book or two, headphones, sunglasses and a few pens. I bought it.

I glanced at the tag as I walked out of the store. It said "Made in China."

Et tu, Vera?

The second locally-born and suckled Fort Wayne company is De Brand Chocolate.

De Brand Chocolate is rich, thick, real chocolate, with rich, thick, real fillings made with cream from flying cows and fruits and nuts tended and harvested by virgins in gauzy white robes with garlands in their spun-gold hair. Each piece of candy is dipped by hand to the music of fairy lutes, and meticulously wrapped in gold foil by enchanted butterflies. You won't find De Brand Chocolate in China, although I have no doubt that Chinese spies lurk beneath the windows, disguised as peony bushes, ears pressed to the panes to steal the secret of the candy's über-lusciousness.

It's pricey. But so is the war in Iraq, and De Brand is *so* much better.

Even as I mourned the Cookie Lady, my heart did a loop-de-loop at the sight of the De Brand counter in Fort Wayne International Airport, a beacon of ecstasy between the restrooms and the car rental booths. I dashed over, drooling at the thought of a plump, perfect glace apricot dipped in bittersweet chocolate.

I bent to examine the candy in the display case.

There were no glace apricots.

The clerk saw me hyperventilating and started to dial 911.

"Glace...apricot..." I stammered.

Oh, he said. *Well.* A couple months ago, De Brand decided to sell glace apricots only in boxes of four. He was out of those.

Sorry, he said.

It was just as well that he didn't have a box of four, because no bank would have floated me the necessary mortgage. Even so, I was devastated. I purchased a mocha-filled dark chocolate bonbon as a consolation prize. It was superb.

But it wasn't a glace apricot.

It was also less filling than a glace apricot. I ate it, and I was still starving.

I dragged myself to my rental car and aimed it up the bypass that would take me to the north part of town, where I would be staying.

When I was growing up here, the only things in the north of Fort Wayne were corn and soybean fields and a sports arena called the Coliseum. Now you can't tip a cow up north without smacking a box store or a chain restaurant.

I avoid chain restaurants because their vegetarian fare is hard-scrambled eggs or pasta primavera buried in shredded Colby. But I was starving, and this was Fort Wayne.

I drove past the usual suspects. McDonald's: *no.* Arby's: *no.* Long John Silver: *no.* KFC: *God, no.* Pizza Hut. Fish houses, steak houses, rib houses: *no, no, no and no—*

But hark—in that strip mall, a massive plastic banner: GIANT SALAD BAR.

A brand-new restaurant named the Golden Corral.

I parked and went in. I collected a tray, plate, utensils, and marched up to the salad bar. It was indeed GIANT—55-gallon drums of lettuce and acres of Midwestern Comfort Food: syrupy mandarin oranges, baco-bits, fifteen varieties of mild cheese, three-bean salad, potato salad, deviled eggs.

But there were also nuts, sunflower seeds, raisins, tattered broccoli nubs and bits of browning cauliflower. I found a low-fat compound among the vats of dressing, drizzled it over my GIANT salad and bore it to my table.

For the Golden Corral, the GIANT SALAD BAR was a come-on. Its real specialty was an all-you-can-eat entrée counter, groaning with beef, pork, cheesy-fries, deep-fried onion rings and jugs of Velveeta sauce. Also, a dessert station the size of Moldova, dedicated to pies.

As I picked at my salad, the clean-up lady deposited a stack of three empty plates on my table for future helpings. "Will that be enough?" she asked.

"That's more than enough," I said.

"Oh," she said. "You'll need more? No problem."

"Come on—who on earth could eat four helpings at a sitting?"

She set down a basket with two buns in it that had been dipped in something orange and greasy. "You're kidding," she said.

I glanced around. The dining room was full.

Everybody in it was…GIANT. GIANT people at tables; GIANT people at the food counters. GIANT people filling trays snugged into GIANT bellies. GIANT old people; GIANT young people. GIANT babies.

Once again it hit me, as it always does when I come to Fort Wayne: *I'm not in New York City anymore.*

Let me be honest: I've lost and regained my full body weight five times in my life. I'm a vegetarian, but chocolate cake is vegetarian. I know that *fat* does not mean *lazy*; nor, conversely, does *slim* mean *industrious*. If that were true, Oprah would weigh 95 pounds.

So I mean no value judgment when I say that the human scenery in Fort Wayne can be jarring. I am not myself thin; I am in no way discomfited by large people. But great rumbling herds of GIANT people, bellying up to an all-you-can-eat buffet: *that* gets my attention.

Self magazine once pronounced Fort Wayne one of the "least fit cities in the US." There is no Fort Wayne triathlon; no footrace up the steps of the Lincoln Tower. You don't see joggers in the

Fort. You don't even see walkers, because there are no sidewalks.

You see cars. Cars, cars, cars, with free parking everywhere and a million drive-through everythings. Marathon, in the Fort, is just another gas station.

Might there be a correlation between this and the scene at the Golden Corral?

I glanced around the restaurant, then down at my GIANT salad. I wasn't starving anymore.

I left my stack of empty plates for the clean-up lady and slipped out of the restaurant, powered across the wide parking lot and into WalMart, where I bought an apple.

[2009]

The Surgeon's Little Helpers

Military hospitals in Viet Nam performed all kinds of surgeries. We had surgeons from every specialty: general surgery, orthopedics, ear-nose-and-throat, eye, even plastic.

In my year in-country, I saw heroic, sophisticated, complex procedures: abdominal resections, surgery performed on beating hearts, work on the nerves and tendons of hands, countless expertly-performed amputations. These procedures were done under less than ideal conditions. Most wounds came to us horribly dirty. It was always hot in the operating rooms, even though they were air-conditioned. Air filtration was an impossible dream. There were, inevitably, flies.

The most common operation we performed was not a dramatic miracle surgery, but an unsophisticated procedure called *debridement*. It was what you did when your patient had been wounded by a fragmentation grenade or a land mine, something that destroyed a lot of tissue in areas outside the sealed, sterile body cavities. Something that packed the wounded areas with dirt, metal bits, and bone shards.

During our basic medical training at Fort Sam Houston, Texas, we were told that this sort of wound was the *object* of modern weaponry. If you kill a man, you eliminate one soldier; if you wound a man gravely but not fatally, you eliminate more because others stop fighting to move their injured buddy from the field. Compassion is a strategic disadvantage.

Accordingly, the guns we used, M16s, were designed to complicate injuries. The munitions experts at Fort Sam assembled us at the firing range and shot an M16 round into a target that was a bone encapsulated in a thigh-sized mold of firm gelatin.

They showed us the entry wound—a neat, bullet-sized hole in the front of the mold—and the exit wound, which was a fist-sized deficit in the rear. The round entered and expanded, shattering the bone. The bone became its own internal fragmentation grenade, exploding small, sharp pieces through the softer tissue behind it.

The VC and the NVA got the same desired effect from their AK47s. Our combat hospitals received many, many young soldiers, both US and Vietnamese, who had massive tissue damage. We received many, many Vietnamese civilians—male, female, young, old—who suffered similar injuries because they accidentally wandered between a weapon and its target. Or, perhaps, because they *were* the target. We seldom knew the why of our patients; we just worked on them. Day and night; night and day.

This is what we did when we met a perfect war wound, a gaping hole packed with clotted blood and gritty red clay, the flesh in shreds: First, we flooded the hole with saline, washed it with surgical soap, flooded it with more saline, painted it with Betadine solution, and draped it in sterile covers—covers much cleaner than the wound itself. Then, all of us who were not needed to hand instruments or hold retractors—doctors, nurses and techs—took up heavy sterile scissors called "Mayos" and cut away the dead tissue.

This was *debridement.*

We snipped away bits of muscle until we reached tissue that twitched when cut, which meant it was alive. We trimmed limp blood vessels until we reached those that bled—they were alive. These, the surgeon—or the nurse—would tie off.

We pulled out bits of metal or stone or dislodged bone or dirt as we went, while the patient slept under the anesthesia mask. Since the wounds were filthy, we gave high doses of antibiotics with the patient's IV fluids.

Also, since the wounds were filthy, we seldom closed them during the first operation.

Instead, once we cleared the dead tissue, we packed the open wounds with gauze. We began by laying a sterile gauze sponge, soaked with sterile saline, on the debrided area, right on the open flesh. Then, we packed more gauze, fluffy fistfuls of it, on top of that, filling the hole. Finally, we wrapped the whole thing in rolls of spongy gauze Kerlix bandages. We might wrap a sterile ace bandage over it all to hold everything secure. Then we'd tape it all together.

We sent the patient wherever he was supposed to be sent. Sometimes, if his other injuries warranted it—head, spinal, other wounds we were not equipped to treat—we'd evacuate him, usually to Japan. If there was no rush to send him out, we'd send him *in*, to one of our own surgical wards.

Later, we'd bring him back in for further debridement. We'd put him to sleep, and cut off all that bulky bandaging we'd put on him the last time.

That was when, in many cases, we found the maggots.

The first time I saw maggots in a wound, white, plump, squirming under the stained gauze, I nearly vomited. The doctor who was operating merely said, "Ah—the Surgeon's Little Helpers."

This was his explanation:

Maggots are the larvae of flies. However, unlike the flies that spawned them—who've been in some truly disgusting places—maggots are not a source of filth in themselves. In fact, they're clean, newly-hatched, quite virginal. But in order to live, they must eat what we consider filth—in this case, dead tissue.

We, too, removed dead tissue; we and the maggots worked toward the same goal.

Alas, maggots, being maggots, get no respect. We summarily washed them from the wound and disposed of them with the old bandages. Then we re-trimmed the dead flesh.

Depending upon the relative cleanliness of what came out of our mutual efforts, we either re-packed the wound, or sewed it up. Many wounds, even once they were clean, could not be sewn up because they had to be covered with skin grafts, which were usually done elsewhere. Others could be closed—a surgeon, for example, might sew a flap of live flesh over the bone once an amputation wound was clean.

The wonder was that so many men with so much trauma managed to live. It helped that they were young, and that they were usually in excellent condition, well-fed and fit. It helped that medevac teams—pilots and staff who manned the huey helicopters painted with red crosses that airlifted the injured from the battlefield—were daring and quick. It helped that doctors were efficient and competent, and that nurses and techs were well-trained. And that we all worked so well together to save these men.

Too often, after all that work on the part of so many people, once a patient had been hospitalized, debrided, sewn up and released, he was sent back into battle. Which made many of us wonder what the point of this whole exercise might be.

Consider: This barbaric procedure of debridement required hours of expensive hospital time. It required thousands of dollars in medical supplies—linens, anesthesia gases and chemicals, disposable gloves, blades and sutures, gauze, IV gear and bottles of solutions, blood, antibiotics, saline, soaps, Betadine, unguents, etc. It required the ministrations of at least one surgeon—whose time would be like gold back in the States—and an absolute minimum of two support staff members, one of which was a nurse. And an anesthetist. And it required all this two, three, maybe four times over.

That was just for the hospitalization.

This man was also evacuated from the battlefield by helicopter, which involved a precision piece of aviation equipment, lots of fuel, a trained pilot and crew, emergency medical equipment, drugs and supplies.

So all this time, money and care—all these resources and personnel—are spent making this soldier well once again. And he is sent back into battle. Where, sometimes, he is re-injured. Which starts the cycle over again.

Or he is killed.

In either case, no one has profited. The surgeon added nothing to his store of knowledge; all he did was cut, tie, bandage sew—things he did as an intern or resident. The anesthetist gained nothing. The surgical staff gained nothing. There was no monetary return for spent supplies, no bonus for spent time. The war was not won. The patient lost valuable flesh. Perhaps his valuable life.

Even the Surgeon's Little Helpers were dead.

Seems to me we would've been ahead of the game if we avoided sending the soldier out to get injured in the first place. Unless all we were doing was testing our weaponry.

And hell, you can do that with a bone in a jello mold.

[2000]

How We Paid a Lot of Money to Stand in Line and Not See the President

Three weeks ago, Paul received an email urging him to volunteer to help the Inaugural Committee in Washington, DC, during the President's Big Weekend.

He signed us up.

The email gave no promises that we would be chosen from thousands of prospective volunteers, so we were overjoyed when Paul got a call from a Committee phone-elf asking us to distribute tickets from 2 to 9:30 p.m. on the Saturday before the inauguration.

She told him there would be follow-up emails with more details.

A day passed. Two. No emails.

But…the call really had been *specific*. So I called our favorite DC hotel for a room for Inauguration Weekend, Friday through Monday night.

The price was $50 higher than usual for Sunday and Monday, and the clerk warned me that it was nonrefundable. I took a deep breath and booked it.

The next day, we got a follow-up email: The Committee regretted to inform us that we had *not* been chosen to volunteer for Inauguration Weekend. However, our names would be added to a waiting list.

Paul emailed back for clarification.

A second email arrived: the Committee regretted to tell us that we had *not* been chosen from the waiting list.

Paul emailed back. I emailed an addy called "Questions," which was supposed to serve confused volunteers.

I emailed again. And again.

No reply; nothing. Nothing.

On Friday morning, still unclarified, we took the train to Washington, DC.

Late that night, in our nonrefundable hotel room, I ordered two nonrefundable tickets on-line, a "donation" of $44 each, for the inaugural parade. The tickets entitled us to sit in the bleachers. A splurge—but how many Inaugural Parades would I experience? I'm short; the only thing I see in a crowd at ground-level is shoulders.

We had to pick up the tickets at the DC Convention Center, the place where we'd report as volunteers. If, indeed, we *were* volunteers.

Saturday morning, we stood in line outside the Convention Center. A man handed us an orange plastic card; we went in and stood in line with others holding orange plastic cards until we reached a room, where we stood in line until we reached a table. A man behind the table gave our names to another man; he walked behind a curtain and returned with tickets to the Green Ticket bleacher section.

The men wore tags around their necks that said "Ticket Distribution Volunteer."

In the hall, we buttonholed a woman whose little earpiece with a crinkly cord marked her as a leader. We explained our volunteer dilemma.

She said she could use us: we should come back at 1:30 and tell the coordinator Josie sent us.

We stood in line at the door at 1:30. When at last we found the coordinator, she didn't care that Josie sent us, because our names were already in her computer, entered three weeks ago.

The coordinator gave us "Ticket Distribution" tags and sent us to the ticket room. Where a young woman named Brianna, wearing the leaderly earpiece with a crinkly cord, grabbed us and replaced our tags with tags that read "Security." She hustled us to separate points on a line. The line snaked around the exhibition hall and, ultimately, to a room on the other side.

For the rest of the day, I checked that people had a blue plastic card, which indicated they'd bought tickets through TicketMaster for the parade or one of the official inaugural balls. People with orange plastic cards, which meant they'd bought their tickets directly from the Committee site, went to a different line.

I sent my blue-ticket people down the length of the hall to Paul; he sent them down the width, to another volunteer. This third volunteer sent them around another corner, to a fourth volunteer, who sent them to the ticket room. It was a long, long walk.

At 3 p.m., a great onrush of ticketholders made it a long, long *line*—one that doubled back on itself, *a la* Disney World.

But by 8:30 p.m., only stragglers were left. Many came directly off planes, trains and buses, luggage in tow, desperate to pick up their tickets before 9, after which they became a true donation. Brianna sent us home, our mission accomplished.

On Sunday, we strolled the Mall. The sky was cloudless; the weather warm. Entrepreneurs hawked T-shirts, buttons, Obamacondoms ("Remember the election with your next erection!"). CNN broadcast from a slapped-up booth; tourists craned for a glimpse of Wolf Blitzer and waved at crowd-cams. Elves set up jumbotrons and barricades and plastic flooring for tomorrow's Big Day. The place swarmed with guys with little earpieces attached to crinkly cords.

Monday morning: Showtime. The Mall teemed with humanity. We stood in the shadow of the Washington Monument to watch the inaugural ceremony on a jumbotron. Americana abounded: Dads hoisted babies on their shoulders; children waved flags; families took pictures of each other. Entrepreneurs hawked T-shirts, buttons, Obamacondoms ("A souvenir that's actually fun!"). It was cold and bright and festive, and as Obama laid his hand on the bible, the screen crackled and went black.

The crowd groaned in near unison. The screen pixilated and sizzled to life, then the sound clicked and skipped, recovered, and cut out entirely. The screen strobed on, off, on. Audio returned, ten seconds behind the video.

Obama's inaugural address hitched and blurred like a train announcement, and the video—when it worked—froze and faded.

Paul suggested that Mitt might be scurrying about, pulling plugs.

We—and most everyone else—gave up before the President left the podium.

We set off to claim our piece of the Green Ticket parade bleachers. It was 12:30; the parade was scheduled to step off at 2:30.

"Plenty of time," Paul said.

Except we couldn't get there.

We started at 15th Street. The police sent us up Constitution Avenue to 17th. From there, they sent us past Pennsylvania Avenue, where all the bleachers were set up, to I Street. Then down I to 13th Street, to wait *en masse* for Security to check us through to our Green Ticket zone on Pennsylvania.

In other words, we surrounded the zone, stretching a half-mile trip into a two-mile square (honest: I mapped it out).

Even so, we might have gotten seats before the parade started if Paul hadn't gotten hungry. We stopped to eat. It took a half-hour, from order to exit. "See? Plenty of time," Paul said.

At 1:45, we reached the pack of humanity that stretched from 13th and I to Pennsylvania Avenue. Thousands of us crammed into a half-mile granddaddy-of-all-lines.

Somewhere up front was a tall wire fence and a white Security tent. Two young doctors who'd been working all night stood beside us. They could see the tent. Paul could see the tent. I could see shoulders.

We stood for 15 minutes, moved three feet, stood. Stood for 20 minutes, moved six inches. Stood. Stood. Stood.

At 2:15, one of the young docs texted a friend, a reporter, who told them the President was still speaking at a dinner.

"Let's pray he keeps on talking," said the woman next to me. I agreed: the later the parade started, the better our chance of getting there in time to see Obama wave from his limo. And we *all* wanted to see Obama wave from his limo; it was why we'd come.

"Maybe Biden will speak," said the young doc. "That'd be good for an hour."

At 2:30, we'd inched halfway up the street. Entrepreneurs on the sidewalk hawked T-shirts, buttons, Obamacondoms ("Be a patriot, even on your back!"). The day grew colder. Paul saw the white tent. I saw shoulders. The parade, amazingly, still hadn't stepped off.

At 3:00, the doc's reporter told him the parade had started.

The woman next to me groaned. "Obama's in the front, or the rear?"

"He's in the front," I told her. "It's Santa who's in back of his parades."

Still, there was hope: the start was a long way from us.

A gaggle of gawkers filled a low balcony near us. One of the women pointed toward the parade route. "There's people coming now," she yelled to us all.

We heard motorcycles. Paul craned his neck to see them pass beyond the white tent. The docs saw them as well. I saw shoulders.

"I think that's *him*," the balcony woman yelled. "It's *him!*" Then, "Oops—not him."

At 3:30, we were three rows behind the gate in the tall wire fence when a stern-looking man on the other side pushed it closed. "Aw, man—c'mon! We been here two hours," the guy next to the gate on our side said.

The young docs shook their heads. "I can't believe we drove all this way—"

The stern man inside stood his ground, saying nothing.

The woman on the balcony screamed, "It's HIM!" She fanned herself with her hand. "It's really HIM, and he's out of the car—"

"Can you see him?" I asked Paul.

"No—I can't see beyond the tent."

Far, far away—miles away, a half-world away—just beyond the white tent, on Pennsylvania Avenue, the crowd went wild.

And then, silence.

The stern man on the other side listened to an earpiece attached to a crinkly cord. People started to leave the pack. Somewhere behind us, entrepreneurs hawked T-shirts, buttons, Obamacondoms ("Salute the Big Man like a big man!"). I blew on my frozen fingers.

"Can't you at least let us in to see the rest of the parade?" the man on our side of the gate pleaded.

"I think he's going to open it," one young doc told the other. "He keeps nodding."

"Hunh," said the woman beside me. "He's been *nodding* for the last half-hour. I think maybe he's *on* something, know what I mean?"

Five minutes later, the stern man opened the gate. We stepped in, unzipped our jackets, put our electronics on a table, turned front and back so a guy could wand each of us. Four tables; four wand-ers. For a crowd of thousands.

We zipped up, picked up our phones and cameras, and walked off to the Green Ticket bleachers.

They were not full. Obama was long gone.

[2013]

Notes/Thanks/Whatever

I have a lot of folks to thank for their help with this work. My Writers Group in Brooklyn, Two Bridges, critiqued it for me, as did my writer buddy and fellow vet David Willson, out in Maple Valley, WA.

Blog-masters John Coyne and Marian Haley Beil gave my ramblings a home at http://peacecorpsworldwide.org, a collection of articles by former Peace Corps volunteers who write, when Amazon.com made blogging so unproductive for its authors.

I'd like to thank the places, and the people, who gave me writing space and WiFi for the price of a soy-milk cappuccino: A big Brooklyn shout-out to the Tea Lounge in Park Slope, and Cafe Madeleine and Qathra Coffee Shop in Ditmas Park, where I go to sidestep the distractions of home and hide from the ADD New York streets.

And, of course, there's my supremely supportive husband Paul, who had the good political sense to laugh at my humorous essays (especially when they poked fun at him). And my kids, Kym, Kramer (my book designer) and Kel, and grandkids Grey and Beckett, who sometimes find themselves wandering through my work.

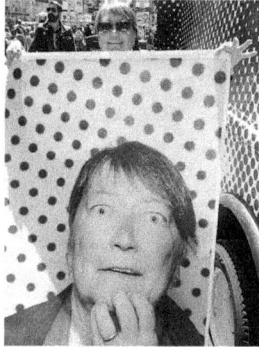

Susan O'Neill is the author of a collection of short stories titled *Don't Mean Nothing*, based loosely on her service as an Army nurse in Viet Nam. An expanded edition is now out in print and electronic editions via Serving House Books. She lives in Brooklyn. Even though you can follow her on Facebook or Twitter (@oneill_Susan), she is on the verge of becoming obsolete.

www.ingramcontent.com/pod-product-compliance
Lightning Source LLC
Chambersburg PA
CBHW060804050426
42449CB00008B/1528